THE OVERLORD EFFECT

EMERGENT LEADERSHIP STYLE AT THE D-DAY INVASION

MICHAEL DAVID PIERCE

authorHOUSE®

AuthorHouse™ UK Ltd.
1663 Liberty Drive
Bloomington, IN 47403 USA
www.authorhouse.co.uk
Phone: 0800.197.4150

Published by AuthorHouse   06/13/2013

ISBN: 978-1-4817-8388-0 (sc)
ISBN: 978-1-4817-8389-7 (hc)
ISBN: 978-1-4817-8390-3 (e)

DEDICATION

This work is dedicated to the memory and spirit
of the men who led the way, fought the good fight, and
sacrificed their lives for freedom in World War II.

ACKNOWLEDGEMENTS

JUST AS IT HAD DONE for the fiftieth anniversary of World War II in the 1990s, the U.S. Army served as the lead agency for commemorating the conflict ten years later. From 2004 to 2005, the Department of Defense World War II Committee organized and hosted the *D-Day 60* events and many other commemorative activities. Major General David T. Zabecki, the 7th Army Reserve Command Commander who had earned a Ph.D. in History, was the officer in charge of the commemorations in Europe. While serving as his executive officer, I had the privilege of being closely engaged in these events, coordinating matters from Normandy to Belgium to Prague, and I transcribed some of the veteran interviews. Assisting with historical aspects of this operation was the late Dr. Charles E. Kirkpatrick, a highly respected historian at Headquarters, V Corps in Heidelberg, Germany. Before his untimely passing, he rendered considerable help transcribing veteran interviews and as a WWII consultant. Moreover, he arranged to get the help of a former V Corps assistant historian, Lieutenant Colonel Alan R. Koenig, Field Artillery, USAR, to transcribe many of the interviews. A military history instructor at the University of Nebraska—Omaha, Dr. Koenig leveraged help from his most talented students to complete the laborious task of transcribing several dozen interviews. These students included: Lisa Zafirov, Mike Jimerson, Tera Smith, Erin Livingston, and Jonathan Melvin.

Summarizing several accounts was Sergeant Ken Hall, a member of the DoD WWII Commemoration Committee.

The U.S. Army Center of Military History at Fort McNair supported the interviewing process, which occurred just up the hill from Omaha Beach, by dispatching Dr. Patrick Hughes and the 44th Military History Detachment, the only active duty unit of its kind in the US Army, as well as three Reserve Military History Detachments that participated in this project: the 49th MHD, and the 305th MHD and 53rd MHD of the 99th Reserve Readiness Center to Normandy to interview the veterans (Hanselman, 2005). The unit interviewed over two hundred veterans attending the commemoration ceremonies.

Members of my dissertation committee spent many hours helping me complete this endeavor. They include:

Dr. Michael G. Bemben
Dr. Trent E. Gabert
Dr. Jorge L. Mendoza
Dr. Susan Sharp
Dr. David T. Zabecki (MG Retired)

The combined labors of all of these people helped to preserve memories of the men who fought in Normandy. Using this support, I discerned lessons in leadership to teach future generations to persevere even when the odds seem impossible, to appreciate the freedom they have, and to understand the price that warriors sometimes must pay to achieve it.

TABLE OF CONTENTS

FOREWORD

OPERATION OVERLORD, THE ALLIED INVASION of the Third Reich's *Fortress Europa*, has received considerable historical coverage. Moreover, on the 60th anniversary of the Normandy invasion, historians of the U.S. Army's Center of Military History, supplemented by members of the 44th Military History Detachment and three other units, the 49th, the 305th, and the 53[rd,] interviewed nearly 200 invasion veterans. These interviews yielded considerable historical material that allowed a qualitative study of American leadership in Normandy in late spring 1944. These oral histories reveal that compelling circumstances activated a core set of leadership competency traits in most of the troops. Other postwar leadership theories simply do not apply for Normandy operations.

I observed leadership behaviors applicable when put to the test of real life combat situations, where making decisions on the Normandy Beaches and in the countryside resulted in people living or dying. The measure of this qualitative study was the observations of whether a core of leadership traits, skills, training, and experience or other factors was present in the examples set by those who participated in D-Day.

The outcome of this research showed that a core of leadership competencies emerged in the American troops, regardless of their background, in times of crisis. Using the knowledge gained from both individual and collective histories of the group studied, this book will present many of the critical factors that enabled leadership to emerge among the participants in the fog of war.

STUDYING D-DAY TO UNDERSTAND EMERGENT LEADERSHIP THEORY

THIS BOOK IS ABOUT LEADERSHIP in action from the vantage point of the men who landed on the beaches of Normandy, France and broke through the vaunted defenses of the Third Reich. Students in leadership will learn much about what causes leadership in action to emerge. I prepared this book to provide a practical leadership primer for young, developing leaders and their mentors. The goal is to provide leadership accounts, discussion of current leadership theories, and constructive examples of how the two fit together. This book provides not only the examples of how leadership can emerge in multiple settings, but also challenges the reader to look for such examples in their own experience and see how they can take their own leadership to a higher level.

Later in the book I introduce emergent leadership theory. This theory discusses how most people will demonstrate leadership when placed in circumstances where their natural innate characteristics will react under the catalyst of a critical life or death event.

Whether one is a soldier, a business professional, or a leader of a non-profit organization, lessons learned from D-Day and the Overlord Effect can be successfully applied in many situations and be used to train and develop better leaders and teams, resulting in a more effective organization, a higher likelihood of personal success for both leaders and followers, and a greater overall improvement in how leaders are selected and groomed.

CHAPTER 1

INTRODUCTION: THE D-DAY INVASION AND ITS RELEVANCE TO LEADERSHIP STUDIES

STUDYING LEADERSHIP THROUGH THE INTERVIEW process has a long standing historical precedent. During World War II, historians interviewed many veterans, and afterward produced several dozen volumes of scholarly works on the war colloquially known as the "Green Books."

The *WWII 60* historians interviewed people who were involved in the war, including civilians, although most of them military personnel. They inquired about a number of topics, including, training, logistics, and weapons. For the study discussed in this book, the key question was: *What was the type of leadership that was displayed during those critical hours, days and weeks that spanned the Normandy Invasion?*

I conducted what is called a descriptive case study of the histories of the D-Day 60 Veterans and acquired a better understanding of leadership theory, identified trends in leadership during crises, and developed a broader understanding and improved theoretical knowledge for understanding and developing leadership. Using examples from the oral histories, I looked for different patterns of leadership approaches that emerged in life and death, combat, and high-intensity training situations. Using modern theoretical approaches in leadership discussion, as well as my own leadership theory framework, I analyzed the situation and present the results in this work.

CHAPTER 2

THE LONG ROAD TO THE NORMANDY LANDINGS

IT WAS GERMAN FIELD MARSHALL Erwin Rommel who first described the 6th of June 1944 as "The Longest Day." Wielding combined forces of 2,876,000 soldiers, sailors and airmen, along with 11,000 aircraft and ships, the Allies attacked. Nearly 200,000 soldiers swarmed ashore in the initial days and weeks of the Normandy Campaign (Stokesbury, 1980; Brinkley, 2006). The objective was only about twenty-five miles across the English Channel. Nearly a millennium earlier, Duke William had left this same area to conquer England in 1066.

On a visit there in 2007, I was struck by the irony of this when I read an inscription at Bayeux that the English, who William of Normandy conquered, returned to liberate it from Nazi Germany. The primary Allied leaders at D-Day included General Dwight D. Eisenhower (the Supreme Commander), General Omar Bradley (the G.I.'s General), Brigadier General Teddy Roosevelt, Jr., who died on the beaches of a heart attack after gallantly leading his soldiers ashore in the fight and directing operations under fire, and Sir Bernard Law Montgomery (Monty), the colorful and sometimes vexing British General. Against them was fortress Europe, with its many cliffs, barbed-wire and hedge rows, all covered by gun emplacements, along the French coast. Invading this hornets' nest was a daunting prospect, involving elaborate planning and deceptions. Indeed, one of America's most flamboyant generals, George S. Patton, posed as commander of a fictitious field army, replete with troops wearing its purported insignia, dummy equipment, and radio transmissions that tricked the German leadership into thinking the Allies could not launch an invasion as early as they did.

The veterans addressed in this study had various roles, and thus differing experiences, in the struggle. Some soared to Normandy in gliders. Others walked ashore and watched comrades cut down as they hit the beach. Many spent the first day on a ship watching the battle, and some had the nightmarish task of filling bins with arms and legs from casualties.

The operation's magnitude was so immense that the Allies towed pre-fabricated harbors to within a mile or so of the beaches. Cargo ships disgorged their contents onto these "Mulberry harbors," and troops drove heavily laden vehicles ashore. The British and Canadian advances on Gold, Juno, and Sword beaches went reasonably well, and the American and French landings on Utah Beach cost about 200 casualties.

In contrast, fierce German fire put the issue in doubt at Omaha Beach, where more than 2400 lives were lost. Ultimately, the Allies gained a foothold, but the subsequent breakout did not come cheaply. Fortunately, the surprised Germans failed to mass their troops, as their planning lacked flexibility to react responsively to the attack, and ultimately the Allies established their foothold.

The first of the five beach locations where the fighting occurred was Sword, by the Orne River on the east flank. The second was Juno, by the town of Courcelles. Next, going further west, was the town of Arromanches, situated between two high bluffs, where Gold Beach was located. The fourth location was Omaha Beach, between Vierville and St. Laurent. Finally, the fifth location was at Utah Beach. It was located just past the Carentan Estuary. Additionally there were two other locations where Invasion troops would be converging—the inland drop site at Sainte-Mère-Église, and the critical glider-borne attack location of Pegasus Bridge.

The invasion caught the Germans napping. Early in the morning of 6 June 1944, paratroopers jumped into the French countryside. Gliders landed and crashed into fields. There followed a heavy bombing of the coast. That morning, when German soldiers looked to the sea, they saw thousands of ships coming in heavily laden with troops, tanks, and supplies.

In a military staff ride there in April 2002, I visited battlefields in and around the countryside in the hedgerows and the beaches. Terrain features proved crucial. The hedgerows defined fields that had been divided and then re-divided by the Norman descendants of the Vikings who moved into the territory during the reign of Charles II, grandson of Charlemagne. Thus, the land of the men from the North was named Normandy. The Norman countryside is unique from the rest of France. The divided lands passing from fathers to sons were reinforced with hedgerows to keep in and preserve the soil. The land has stayed in families for generation upon generation. Therefore, the countryside during World War II was dotted with small square fortresses all around.

This made the fighting especially difficult because it obscured the enemy until it was upon the Allied tanks. Also, when the Allied tanks went over the hump of the hedgerow, the bellies of their tanks were exposed and vulnerable to attack. The Allies had to go from hedgerow to hedgerow for miles, cleaning out enemy forces. This process took several weeks.

The only way to get into the countryside was by way of the Allies clearing the beaches. The terrain was uphill from the beach. Much of it was high cliffs. Only a few spots along the coastline in the area were suitable to drive up out of the water and uphill. These spots were clearly identified by the German defenders who mined and wired the beaches and built iron and cement barriers to create a seemingly impregnable obstacle course. Overlooking the beaches was artillery with range enough to reach the ships at sea. To get past the waterline, one had to traverse several hundred meters in full battle gear.

On my visit, I ran from the low tide mark up the beach to where the grass line was at Omaha Beach. Imagining the bullets, noise, chaos, and obstacles the liberators experienced showed me the enormity of the task these soldiers faced.

Allied troops make their way ashore on June 6, 1944
Source: http://docs.fdrlibrary.marist.edu:

In late summer 2007, I walked along the beach at Arromanches, France, with my wife and children. The tide was out, and the Mulberry harbor remnants from the great invasion were easily accessible by foot. One can still touch the massive objects that served as a giant bridge from the sea. The sandy beach gives way to rocks as one approaches the shore line, and a deteriorating gun emplacement still commands a hill on the far right.

The oral histories of the men who were there add a new richness to the story of D-Day. Using a broad theoretical base to examine it today, we can look at their actions in a new light and develop a deeper appreciation of not only the history but also the character of the men who fought there, as well as the impact their leaders had on them. There is no doubt that if the leadership had failed, then the invasion would have been a disaster.

The Normandy campaign was a resounding success due to the ineptitude of the German high command and the successful application of better leadership at the top among the Allied Generals.

In the military, there are three levels of conflict: the *strategic* level, the *operational* level, and the *tactical* level. Germany had over-extended its resources at the strategic level by going too far, too fast, without the resources to maintain them. On the operational level, German leadership failed to provide adequate resources to commanders when they needed them, and this resulted in battles that led to additional lost resources. Leadership issues at the top of the German staff, where Hitler had been too involved for years, resulted in a failure of the highest magnitude for Germany's forces. Earlier in the War, similar leadership deficiencies in the Soviet Army had given the Germans an early advantage. However, political appointees and party favorites of Stalin were soon replaced by more competent generals.

Leadership at the operational and strategic level was important. But, the tactical leadership on the ground was also a critical factor. General Matthew B. Ridgway was one of the leaders at D-Day. His leadership and vision made him an archetype for a transformational leader. A transformational leader is one who engages with others and raises the level of both morality and motivation in followers and leaders. Ridgway led the 82d Airborne Division and ensured his troops were trained and capable soldiers who could do the mission. "Ridgway was a solid man; (there was) nothing phony about him," Major Dick Winters was quoted as saying: (While) talking with his troops (he) had everyone's respect. (There was) never any doubt on (his) character, manhood or leadership."

Winter's description of Ridgway as a man of character, with the ability to gain people's respect thru his honesty and integrity, exemplified critical leadership traits, and these proved necessary for success at that level. Moreover, one must wonder how much these traits trickled down to the soldiers by example, or, were they already part of their character?

Ridgway left a strong cadre of leaders at the 82nd's base in England to train replacement troops while the rest of the unit was in Normandy. In so doing, the cadre emphasized and built tradition into their character. His insistence on a strong tradition, a focus on basic skills and conditioning, remained in effect, as the 82d Airborne Division not only went on to success at D-Day but also serves as the preeminent division in the Army today. Thus, a strong leader can effect an organization in the long term as well as the short.

Before he assumed command of the 82nd, Ridgway had benefited from General Omar Bradley's tutelage. This may have been crucial, as the latter's moniker was "the GI's General," a nickname bestowed upon him by the famous war correspondent Ernie Pyle. Thus, the Army's very nature employed a veritable chain of leadership, not just in the hierarchical sense, but in the sense of passing tacit knowledge, sharing values, and creating conditions for success.

Bradley and Ridgeway served well at the top, but did the men they led have the same character and values? Under different circumstances, might they also have become division commanders? Impressions left by the leaders at an organization's apex can inspire others to follow them, but they do more to catalyze that *seed* of leadership. For those who make it through the early challenges of leadership development, this results in successful leaders who do not act as "buffalo" when the leader falls.

D-Day veterans certainly did not stop what they were doing and wait for the top buffalo to emerge. Countless examples appeared where the mission continued without skipping a beat when leaders fell. Many of the soldiers who displayed this leadership had benefited from the transformational leadership of men like Ridgway and Bradley. *Transformational* leadership brings both the follower and leader to a higher level of morality, and results in an intrinsically higher motivation coupled with similar performance results.

Consider Corporal Duke Boswell of the 505th Parachute Infantry Regiment (PIR) He did not follow the paradigm that if the lead buffalo falls, the herd sits. Instead, he took charge and led his soldiers until they met up with the rest of the unit.

> I landed just north of the Ste Mere Eglise Church. Since I jumped first through the door, I had to go in a particular direction to round up the rest of the guys. We had a small flashlight on a pole I put together to help others find both myself and others I grouped with within minutes of landing. (Boswell)

This is one example of how these soldiers would successfully perform because of the leadership that had nurtured them. They did not stop functioning because the commander was not there to tell them what to do. Studying the oral histories of the D-Day veterans 60 years after the battle gives us the opportunity to see the follower and the leader, as well as to get a sense of what some of those who were impacted by leadership of the time did afterwards. Many of the veterans who were interviewed at the D-Day 60 Commemorations were from the 82d Airborne Division. Others were from the 101st Airborne, and the 4th Infantry and 29th Infantry Divisions. Some of the veterans arrived immediately or soon after the event. In some cases, the veterans included in the accounts had served in different locations, but their accounts provided a unique insight for their situation, while at the same time, demonstrating that the actions and leadership displayed at D-Day were not limited only to that day and location. Their words speak volumes about the impact of leadership, tradition, and character at the individual level during one of the most important military campaigns of World War II.

CHAPTER 3

HOW D-DAY UNFOLDED: THE VETERAN'S PERSPECTIVE

Aspects of the Invasion

A PARTIAL CHRONOLOGY OF D-DAY, Operation Overlord, is given here according to the accounts of the men in our study group who participated in the invasion and witnessed it firsthand. The veterans interviewed were not historians, and there are some inaccuracies in the interviews regarding caliber of weapons, or ranks and names of persons mentioned. I doubt that 60 years after my tour in Iraq I will be able to recall all the details about the type of weapons and vehicles in use. The chronology is not complete, but it does give a good picture of much of what went on during Operation Overlord from the participants' viewpoints. More importantly, it shows the breadth of the sample: soldiers, sailors, airmen, enlisted, non-commissioned officers, junior officers, partisans. Even the recollections of a German soldier are included.

The accounts presented here in our limited chronology are only a small fraction of the thousands that have been taken and preserved by historians. The accounts show many aspects of Operation Overlord. Several of the accounts provided direct examples of leadership in action. Other examples showed indirectly what leaders (and followers) felt or saw. As mentioned earlier, this section is not a complete history of Operation Overlord. It is a snapshot of various personal experiences of the men who were there to provide a framework for studying the operation from a theoretical leadership perspective. Countless books, articles, and movies have been written about Overlord's historical importance. There were many errors in the historical facts in the accounts. These were addressed as much as possible. However, this does not diminish the main points or the value of the accounts themselves. The veterans did not have their notes with them, nor did they have the time (most of them) to sit and write it all down as it happened. They all experienced these events, and whether they got the facts straight or not is less important in this discussion than what they took from their experience of being at, or taking part in D-Day, Operation Overlord. It is the impression that these events left on them and the leadership that we will be focusing on as it is discussed and analyzed. Some accounts refer to events that follow D-Day, and in a few cases, there are accounts of events that did not take place there. But in all cases the accounts are from WWII Veterans who attended one of the many World War II 60th Anniversary commemorative events. This book is an examination of leadership during a crisis, using the accounts of these veterans.

The men studied in these accounts all had different experiences; but the leadership they observed and displayed at various times often proved to be the difference between life and death.

CPT Ralph Goranson had to lead his men up the cliffs and then face the enemy on the high ground, going through the networked trenches that made up the German defense. His critical mission enabled success for the men who hit the beaches because it prevented the Germans from using part of their transportation network.

Similarly, Derek Fearon and the men at Pegasus Bridge affected German movements and prevented reinforcements from getting to the beaches area.

Another example given here of the kind of leaders studied was Pierre Collard, whose Maquis resistance fighters so harried a German SS Division in another part of France, that it arrived too late to reinforce the beaches and towns of Normandy.

Together, these men, and all of the others fighting at Normandy were part of a greater effort that slowly, but thoroughly, chipped away at and eventually broke through the wall that kept the Allies out of Hitler's Fortress Europe. Many of them never made it beyond the beaches of Omaha or Utah, or past their drop zones around Sainte-Mère-Église and Sainte-Marie-du-Mont. Some men were captured, others fought all the way through to the end of the war and saw its worst atrocities.

The accounts described leadership experienced from the lowest level—such as between two comrades of equal rank—to the first line squad leaders and NCOs leading the way, and on up to the level of the officers leading platoons and companies. They presented a commentary on organizational level leadership as well, such as that described in the Slapton Sands incident by Harold McCauley.

I. Prelude: Aerial reconnaissance

A good reconnaissance can determine success or failure of a military operation. Maps and information from people familiar with Normandy helped, but the Allies needed to supplement such information with aerial photography to contribute to the mosaic that gave intelligence analysts a textured image of what the invaders faced. At the same time, the Allies had to reconnoiter Normandy in a way that would not make the *Oberkommando der Wehrmachts* (the German High Command) suspicious that frequent over-flights heralded an invasion. Returning from bombing Cherbourg, Milton Abernathy had orders to fly over the invasion beaches late in 1943. He had no idea he was flying a reconnaissance mission of the Normandy countryside that analysts later used to plan the invasion.

I served with the 303rd Bomb Group, 358th Bomb Squadron, Army Air Force. On the 31st of December 1943, we went on what we were told was a bombing run to Bordeaux, France to attack a ship at an altitude of 16,000 feet. After flying through clear skies, we arrived at our objective but the ship was missing. We did not run into any opposition and enjoyed good visibility to Cherbourg, where we saw the beaches. On a good day at 16,000 feet, you can see a lot, but not the little things.

On the way back our group leader ordered a 360 degree turn around Cherbourg, thus we covered the whole of Normandy and returned very late. We looked in the bombers' bomb bays and found they carried lots of cameras; most of our planes were just taking pictures. We mused we may have been some kind of decoys for the Bordeaux run.

The 360 degree turn allowed us to cover most of the beaches and when we came around from Cherbourg, we turned back east and over London even though it was getting dark. We were barely able to land in the dark for our New Year's party, which none of us felt like attending since the long flight had exhausted us. A week later, we learned our bomber carried the cameras to examine potential landing beaches for invading the continent. (*On a Clear Day You Can See Forever: 303rd's Milton Abernathy's New Year's Eve Party at 16,000 Feet*—(Summarized by SGT Kenneth Hall)

Another key aspect of the prelude to invasion was the prerequisite training that involved rehearsing several divisions' moves to the coast, boarding ships, landing, and maneuvering in a war zone. This training was realistic but cost many lives. Harold McCauley spoke of Exercise Tiger, one of the costliest training debacles of the entire war. The Allied invasion was only weeks away, but critical synchronization of troop, air and sea movements was incomplete. This confusion, coupled with a coinciding attack by German U-boats, led to the deaths of hundreds of Allied troops, who drowned because their Landing Ship Tanks (LST) were sunk. The British naval support for the training exercise was inadequate due to several critical errors in communication between the British and American military. McCauley drove a self-propelled amphibious vehicle. Not only did he participate in the training exercises, but he also literally fished bodies out of the water with other crew members. Additionally, they had to spend time in confinement after the exercise so that word of the loss of life during the training event did not leak to the press.

I was in *"Exercise Tiger,"* the mock invasion at Slapton Sands, England. We were not briefed until the night of the exercise. The British were supposed to be our escort. I had been in three invasions, so at four o'clock I told my sergeants we lacked escorts. The British left, and we had no protection . . . They must have sunk the ship I was on a few minutes after I got off and it put back out on the water. They classified me as a survivor after that . . . they kept it quiet for forty years and made us swear that we would not say anything or we would get court-martialed if you were in the service. I don't know what they could do if you were milking cows, but it was kept secret for forty years.

I was in charge of three DUKWs [Author's Note: a six-wheel-drive amphibious truck]. One guy had been in the engineers, and had been in every outfit in the Army. He ended up in our outfit because there was only one place worse than our unit, and that was the gliders. If we could not handle them, they went to the gliders. We got into a fight. I was his corporal and he said something to me. I broke his nose and he broke my nose. Somehow, we ended up as the best buddies that ever was. We got together at the reunions and cried every time.

We didn't know what was going on. The Navy was supposed to fire naval guns that night. We thought that was it. We could see and hear all the noise. Pretty soon the water caught fire . . . A guy I knew, his name was Dwight Coles from Branch, Arkansas . . . and I took DUKW's out to look for *floaters* . . . bodies of dead Americans floated in the water after the landings. We called them that because they floated with their butts in the air and their heads down. We had to look at their dog tags as they all looked the same.

There was a bulldozer that came up ahead of me to this pill box. The small caterpillar dug a trench, and we buried a lot of Americans in it, but nobody would admit it and they called Cole and I liars. They closed the hatches of the LST's during the attack. A few guys got out. They are still in the channel with a lot of equipment out there.

I knew too much about burying the dead after Slapton Sands. One general committed suicide over it. They were keeping us quiet about what had really happened. They put us behind barbed wire for fourteen days, with guards on us in seven-man tents. I can't tell you where it was in England, but there was a castle not far from us.[1] (*Slaughter at Slapton Sands*—(Summarized by SGT Kenneth Hall, edited by Dr. Alan Koenig)

---

[1] During Exercise Tiger two German E-boats came upon the exercise and slipped in and sank two of the LSTs and severely damaged a third. It was critical to maintain this as secret until after the invasion itself because making it public would have completely blown the cover of the invasion (Zabecki, 2009).

II. Bringing in the airborne attack

Besides amphibious operations, the Allies delivered troops to Normandy by gliders and by cargo planes. The gliders were towed by C-47s, and were designed to land along with their troops in the Normandy countryside. The paratroopers would jump into what were hoped to be the right pre-designated drop zones. As the accounts suggest, the air drops were not very precise in many cases. This resulted in troops being scattered throughout the hedges and fields below. The gliders that landed stealthily around Pegasus Bridge were a fortunate exception to the norm, and their troops secured the bridge with light casualties.

The next series of accounts illustrate the invasion's first few hours from the perspective of the men who delivered the warriors. In so doing, the invaders displayed uncommon courage just to get into some of the light craft, unarmored aircraft, and gliders, which had to land in foreign fields at night.

Frederick Crispin and Robert Dains were navigators in the C-47 aircraft that brought troops over the landing zone around Sainte-Mère-Église. They were part of a massive air armada that crossed the English Channel in the early morning hours of D-Day. Crispin arrived in England in January of 1944. He was in a troop carrier squadron. He and his fellow pilots flew in to Normandy from Southampton. Their course took them through the Jersey-Guernsey islands, where they made a ninety degree turn that took them to their destination. Crispin, a second lieutenant and aerial navigator provides the following description of his mission:

> The weather was rotten. We come across from Southampton at twelve hundred feet. By the time we got to the French coast, the Jersey Islands, we were down to a thousand feet and lowering. By the time we made the turn in we were at eight hundred feet, and by the time we got to the drop zone, we dropped them at seven hundred feet . . . I dropped the 505th (PIR), 82nd. Those men were magnificent. Buddy, the spirit of those guys . . . when they got in that airplane on the night of the 5th they were so heavy with equipment. When they went up on that back door into the C-47 you had to help them in, that's how loaded they were. Good troops! I mean they were super troops. (*Frederick Crispin, Army Air Corps*

Navigator, 2nd Lieutenant, aerial navigator—(Summarized by
Lisa A. Zafirov, edited by Dr. Alan Koenig)

Flying the gliders was dangerous but necessary. Robert Dains was
a navigator in a C-47 that towed Gliders across the channel for this
mission and describes the touch-and-go aspect:

> On the 6th of June, 1944, I was a navigator on a C-47 that
> pulled a glider into Normandy. We dropped our troopers on
> Sainte-Mère-Église at 1:14 in the morning, and they weren't
> due in until 6:30 in the morning, so we were a little bit ahead
> of things. {Author's Note: Dains is referring to releasing the
> glider infantry into the area, not paratroopers who were
> jumping from other aircraft.}We flew abeam of Cherbourg
> and got a lot of antiaircraft fire. We didn't know for sure what
> we were in for, but we had a job to do and we did it.
>
> We were the seventy-ninth aircraft of an eighty-one ship
> formation, and we saw the show ahead of us well. We almost
> bought the farm twice on that one, but we got through it. On
> D+1 we towed another glider into Normandy, but we had
> nothing inside our plane because the glider's weight was all
> the C-47 could take. For the gliders, it was a one-way trip.
> They worked out well for what they did.

This description of the mood and men on the flight over captured
what was going on in hundreds of gliders and airplanes on 6 June
1944. Derek Fearon landed in a glider at Pegasus Bridge, where troops
fired the battle's first shots. Fearon described the ground invasion's first
hours as he and his fellow British soldiers waited for the relief forces
to link up with them as they held critical bridges that delayed German
reinforcements from reaching the beach area and allowed the Allies to
gain their foothold. British 7th Battalion, The Parachute Regiment, 5th
Brigade, 6th Airborne Division, He helped to secure Pegasus Bridge in
the early morning hours of June 6th. He describes the mission below:

> We lost a lot of men who were dropped in the wrong river
> valley. Of course, the aircraft dropped people in the wrong

places, but they managed to make their way to where they were supposed to be. Eventually, after D+2 or D+3 we were pretty well up to strength. We inevitably deployed 120 men out of a whole battalion.

The role of the parachute and the glider borne, there were three gliders that crash landed on the bridges over the River Orne, and the River Canal, and they did a marvelous job for within twenty minutes, the two bridges had been secured, and we found the demolition charges under the bridges, but fortunately for us the detonators had not been primed and we made it across the bridge.

It was a sheer surprise; but a number of us were still killed as two German panzer tanks had located our movement and probed into us with heavy fire but I don't think they knew exactly what was taking place . . . (*God Save the Queen! British 5th Brigade's Derek Fearon's Bridge Too Far*—(Summarized by SGT Kenneth Hall)

III. Hitting the ground in Normandy

Having left the airplane or glider, the paratroops began their real work at Normandy. The months of training, previous military campaign experience, and abilities of all the men would soon pay dividends as they faced their greatest challenges yet. Men from different units assembled as their planes had scattered them across the countryside. Accordingly, they formed into *ad hoc* squads, fighting when meeting the enemy, hiding when outnumbered, and slowly working their way to rally with other units.

Thomas Alley was in the 101st Airborne Division, serving in the 2nd Battalion, 506th Infantry. He had boarded a ship in September 1943 in New York and headed to Liverpool, England. He was one of the soldiers flown in by men like Frederick Crispin and Robert Dains. Jumping out at a little over seven hundred feet made for a fast descent to the ground, and he could hear the church bells of a French village on the way. He and his compatriots landed miles from their objective and had to gather members of their unit, fight their way to rally points, and continue the fight. They often met troops from other units who joined them for a while, and then sought to join their own units. Alley's account:

> I was with a group of three companies, Dog, Easy and Fox, 2nd Infantry Battalion, 506th Parachute Infantry Regiment. We spent about a week studying maps, especially Pecuville, (Author's Note: Turqueville) and we even knew which building the town mayor was in. Each unit had an assignment, and everybody knew where the enemy positions were, and what we needed to do to take that town.

> I landed in a pasture or vineyard, and had to cut all my parachute gear off. I assembled my M-1 rifle, got my [2]cricket out, and crawled to a hedgerow. I heard a noise and used my cricket. An 82nd Airborne Division sergeant responded. We went around and picked up other 82nd and 101st troops. We heard a sound like squeaking wheels and we all jumped into a ditch. German soldiers with a donkey and a cart made the noise. The sergeant and I jumped out and the five Germans surrendered to us three Americans. The sergeant took the automatic weapon from the first German soldier, but when he went to take the second soldier's weapon, he hit the sergeant across the face with a leather donkey whip. From where I stood four feet away, I shot that guy with my M-1 right in the head and he went down right there. This other guy from the 82nd was still holding the German's automatic weapon and opened up on the other ones who had begun to run and fire at us. We killed the remaining four quickly with their own weapons. We decided to get out of there and began walking down the road. We picked up seven more of our guys a hundred yards or so down that road . . . The 82nd

---

[2] The cricket was a small handheld signaling device used to make a clicking noise. The sign was one click, and the countersign was two clicks. Thousands of soldiers carried the device during the invasion.

paratrooper[3] who was timely with that automatic weapon went another direction with the *All-American* troops that appeared from a field. I never saw him again. (*Two Years in the Making*-(Summarized by SGT Kenneth Hall)

Troops of the 82nd Airborne Division, Ed Asbury, Reuben Breitling, and Carl Hatcher, landed near Sainte-Mère-Église. Before long, they engaged in hand-to-hand combat that showed just how serious things had become. The men experienced the full spectrum of combat at Normandy, complete with war's ironies and contrasts. Some paratroopers narrowly missed being burned alive when they landed among buildings set afire from the earlier bombing runs; but others were not so lucky.

Ed Asbury was a pathfinder and among the very first of the invasion force to arrive. His cargo pockets ripped open during his jump, and he lost most of his ammunition and rations. The harsh reality of combat, danger, and confusion were recurring themes as the men struggled to find comrades, evade the enemy, and accomplish their missions. Once he found his unit at the rally point, Asbury was told to go find the pilots of the gliders and his commander. He took a jeep and found the men and got his commander to an aid station. During this time, his jeep hit a mine and one of his comrades lost an arm in the blast, another man lost his leg and most of his hip. Throughout the ordeal, Asbury remained calm, even repairing a tire that was blown up during the explosion.

> I landed just north of the Sainte-Mère-Église Church. I jumped through the door first, so I had to go in a particular direction to round up the guys. We had a small flashlight on a pole I put together to help others find myself and others with within minutes of landing.
>
> German soldiers appeared around a big burning barn. One of our troopers actually landed in the barn fire, and the Germans wouldn't let the French townspeople pull him out. He died in the flames.

---

[3] Author's Note: The 82nd Airborne is known as the *All-American* Division.

We killed a lot of the enemy who refused to leave the town, and finally pushed the enemy out, and things got quiet for awhile. My unit took control of a key enemy intersection. We kept them from getting down to the beach to reinforce their troops while more of our troops landed and took the pillboxes as the Germans ran out of ammunition and did not get reinforcements.

At about 4:30 a.m., our brigade commander, "Cannonball Krause," [4] declared Sainte-Mère-Église secure. He had been carrying the same flag he had raised in Naples, Italy. He raised it over the town hall. This was the first town that the Allies officially liberated during the D-Day invasion.

After the first twenty-four hours, we didn't know exactly where the enemy was but they were definitely all around us. I remember 42% casualties in the first twenty-four hours of our landing. I think the enemy was as confused as we were, but they didn't seem to be scared of us. (*A Native American's War Dance*—(Summarized by SGT Kenneth Hall)

Reuben Breitling landed in a hen house and met two French girls bearing a bottle of wine, recalling a similar incident in Erich Marie Remarque's powerful anti-war classic *All Quiet on the Western Front* (Remarque, 1929).

On D-Day, I landed two blocks east of Sainte-Mère-Église's center, disturbing a chicken coop in someone's back-yard. Soon, two girls came running outside saying "American" and offered me wine. I told them I had a war to fight but still had some wine and then convinced the girls to go back inside house before I left.

---

[4]   Author's Note: LTC Krause was a Battalion Commander. Some accounts refer to him as the Regimental or Brigade Commander, others describe him as the Regimental Executive Officer, but at D-Day he was the Battalion Commander for 3rd Battalion, 503rd Parachute Infantry Regiment (Zabecki, 2009).

I killed three or four enemy soldiers near the church as they approached me. I stayed in that area about three weeks, and was under fire two-thirds of the time. I remember a German 88 firing at us, seemingly non-stop. (*One Flew 'Onto' the Cuckoo's Nest*—(Summarized by SGT Kenneth Hall).

Others faced more serious situations on the ground. Carl Hatcher was with the Headquarters, 3rd Battalion, 505th Parachute Infantry Regiment. Hatcher commented, "What some called foolish I called opportunity, thus I volunteered to go into all the tough operations coming our way." His unit jumped just outside of Sainte-Mère-Église. They met fierce resistance for several days because the town was a communications center for the Germans. Hatcher describes the leadership of "Cannonball Krause," his battalion commander, and the action going around as the soldiers landed, rallied, and went in to take the town of Sainte-Mère-Église.

Our regimental executive officer, Major Edward Krause, [5] lost his flares (Author's Note: flares would have been used as signals by units to mark assembly points for the troops who were landing.) when he jumped. Luckily, we landed fairly close, for the most part, to where we were supposed to be. Others landed miles away from the *green smoke zone*, northeast of Sainte-Mère-Église.

A barn burned near to where we landed, but we extinguished the blaze and met the French resistance. They wore orange arm bands for identification as Allies, which helped us considerably. The first night after we landed, we killed about a dozen Germans and captured about twenty others.

For the average soldier, the situation seems confusing and chaotic; it's hard to make sense of the things. You're looking over your shoulder and trying to protect yourself and accomplish the mission. While we were still scattered,

[5]   ibid

Major Krause did well at reorganizing us. Having carried an American flag that had flown at Naples, he raised this symbolic banner over the town hall once we took the town. (*82nd's Carl Hatcher Brings Big Action into 'Little Village'* Viva la Resistance! (Summarized by SGT Kenneth Hall)

IV. The sea approach

The invasion force leaving for France had ships and craft of all types and size, from battleships and cruisers, to LSTs (landing ship, tanks), DUKWs, and towed blimps to discourage air attack. Thousands of sailors and seaborne soldiers facilitated this huge logistical undertaking. Delivering the troops and supplies was just part of their job, since the naval craft also had to support the troops ashore, being their only link back to home. Thus, the ships evacuated thousands of wounded on their return journey, and they brought in the massive Mulberry harbors that served as ports until the Allies secured Cherbourg and other facilities. Without them, the Allies would have wasted the airborne and glider-borne troops' gains, since they required a huge influx of troops and supplies to sustain the invasion.

William Dabney was trained to manage the barrage balloons that were used to ward off air attacks on naval vessels used in the invasion. His equipment for his mission was damaged and lost on the way across the channel, but he still was an eyewitness to history. Dabney was a balloon chief in the 320th Barrage Balloon Battalion. This unit was the only African-American combat unit to take part in the initial D-Day landings. As a balloon chief, Dabney was responsible for training his men and deploying the balloons. His account describes the work involved in putting this critical asset to use.

To make the skies above a lucrative target hazardous to an attacker, defenders deployed barrage balloons, which were large captive blimps secured with steel cable capable of destroying or damaging aircraft. Some even carried bombs set to detonate if an aircraft struck the cable. We trained on a much bigger balloon than the one we brought in on the beach. We learned how to inflate, moor, and patch the balloon. We learned how to operate the wench in the strong wind because they would dip and dive ascending or descending. When the wind was strong, we turned the winch slowly to maintain control.

For my crew, there was myself, I was the chief, and my three men. There were four men to a crew. I was the only one in the crew who went to school because I was the one commanding. I told my men what to do. I picked the sites where we would bed the balloon down. I got orders for specific areas and then I needed to find a level spot for the equipment.

Sometimes, while on board the ship we flew the balloon. I think the barge must have been about half a mile out in the English Channel. Before we hit the beach, my balloon got shot out from under me and of course I had to cut the strap because it had a bomb, and it fell to the water because the bomb has to catch the wing of the plane for it to explode and so it must have fallen into the water.

I cut the cord and I came in without my balloon. Incoming fire was pretty strong so when we made it to the beach we literally hit the sand—and stayed there. The tide was coming in so we had to raise our heads above the water. They were scrapping (Author's note: Sweeping the beach looking for mines). Finally, the engineers had cleared enough mines to let us move inland in relative safety. Once we were inland, troops delivered equipment, supplies, more balloons, tanks and other weapons . . . (*Air Defense by Barrage Balloon*—(Summarized by SGT Kenneth Hall, edited by LTC Alan Koenig)

Roy Chilton served with the British Navy. He served on a Mark V landing craft during the Normandy Invasion. He landed with American engineers and endured direct fire from the trenches. Once his craft unloaded the 20 Americans on board, they ran a tape to either side of them to show the passage for follow-on landing craft. The departure was delayed for 24 hours because of rough weather. The American soldiers and their British Navy hosts finally set off for Normandy at 4 o'clock the morning of 6 June, 1944.

We all knew what we were there for, and the Americans were all nice lads. I think that we were all scared when we went over. There were some older ones . . . and we would share a cup of tea and good conversation while we were waiting.

There was a gun on the front end of our Mark V, and I was also trained on that weapon's use. We could hear the German machine guns ahead of us. The only thing that was worrying to me was the beach was being shelled. That was powerfully dangerous.

We got into a trench for several hours, and one of our lads got hit in the leg. We had to stay in there until the sea came in enough to let us go back out. Our injured lad was taken to an American tent for treatment. When the ocean came back in, we pulled out to an American repair ship as we had taken damage. An American repair ship was out in the channel and asked us if we needed assistance, but we couldn't make that connection then so we carried on until later when a British cruiser fired on us as we were not able to signal it to let it know who we were. Since our call sign changed every day, our skipper didn't know the current call sign. We were lucky that they missed us and figured out who we were before they sent us to the bottom. We made it back to England for a short time for repairs and returned to Normandy, but this time it was on a Mark III to Utah Beach. I went into the tents on an American camp. I lined up and had chow with them and the next day, I went to Omaha Beach with the Americans again. I remember a film being shown about Gentleman Jim Corbet and Jack Dempsey and that was an "experience" to be watching that film on a beach just weeks after an invasion of France. (*British Royal Navy's Henry Roy Chilton: LNO to Omaha Beach*—(Summarized by SGT Kenneth Hall)

Few accounts portray the direct effect of a concerned leader better than the Louis Happle and Gordon Howell account of a colonel who personally saw to it that a Medal of Honor nominee would receive prompt and immediate medical care and get safely aboard a medical transport. Happle and Howell met while serving in the Navy. The lifelong friends worked on an LST from 1943 until D-Day. Gordon Howell described their experience at D-Day as they ferried the wounded back and forth from the beach to the USS *Texas*.

> The LST was 327 feet long, and had three Higgins boats (Landing Craft, Vehicle, Personnel (LCVP) on each side. Loading and lowering the boats were not easy tasks, and it took about fifteen minutes to get the troops into them and lower the boats into the water. For the Normandy landings, Happle served as the starboard gunner and Howell was the coxswain on Higgins Boat Number Six They headed to shore after others had already done so. Howell skillfully delivered the troops of the 29th Infantry Division to Omaha Beach's Red Easy area. The Germans had many heavy weapons in the hills just off the beach, and they fired incessantly.
>
> On D+1, Happle and Howell evacuated wounded troops from the beach. Suddenly, a jeep arrived and a colonel got out and helped a wounded staff sergeant toward the Howell's boat. Both men were from the 101st Airborne Division. Howell's LST had three doctors and about twenty corpsmen on board, but the colonel asked him how long it would take to get to the USS *Texas* off the coast, and he replied about a half-hour. The colonel said that wasn't fast enough. At the time, five or six Higgins boats evacuated wounded from the beach with Happle and Howell's boat. The colonel and the wounded sergeant got on board their boat, and Howell headed for the *Texas*. He approached a gangway, and a sailor said, "This is an officer's gangway, you can't pull up here." The colonel replied, "Young man, let me tell you something—I have a wounded man here that I am putting in for the Medal of Honor, and I don't want to hear anything about gangways. I want him brought up there right now!" A naval officer hastened to the scene and took the staff sergeant on board. It was the only soldier Happle and Howell ever saw taken to a battlewagon for treatment. (*Shipmates Gordon Howell and Louis Happle on Course*—(Summarized by SGT Kenneth Hall, edited by LTC Alan Koenig)

Normandy Beach Area, June, 1944
Source: National Archives Photo # 26-G-2517

V. Sea landings

Despite the short distance between England and France, the sea journey lasted several hours. By the time the men arrived all packed and ready to hit the beaches, many had become seasick and soaked to the bone. When the invasion fleet drew near and the LSTs deposited their cargo, there were no wharves, docks, or gangways to cross. There was only the sea, barriers, mines, and automatic fire coming from well-defended positions to greet the invaders. The men had to wade through water that had treacherous sink holes, also called ruttles, where many men lost their lives. Others were gunned down within steps of leaving the water craft. Some water craft never made it to the shore, taking whole tank crews to the watery depths with them. The accounts in this section give a partial feel of the fight from the landing craft onto the beaches.

The troops poured ashore, their comrades falling around them. From Omaha Beach to Utah Beach, each unit had to overcome challenges. Charles Arcieri provided signal support under fire as troops came onto the beach. He was more worried about losing a limb than getting killed. In his account, he shared some surprising insights about what a young man is thinking while under fire.

> In the days leading up to D-Day, we spent our time loading and getting things to work right before we packed everything for the LST to the beachhead.
>
> We landed in the pre-dawn hours of D-Day . . . Once we hit the sand, there wasn't much difficulty getting communications set up. We were responsible for the transmitters. Morse code guys would run this equipment. The biggest concern was certain types of gear burning up or breaking down, like the generators, and the quality of the gas we used for the generators.
>
> Even more of a potential problem was in the constant securing of that bunker on Normandy beach where we landed to set up all the communications arrays to keep the ships in contact with the command elements of the land forces. My biggest concern was that I might lose an arm or a leg and not be able to do my duty. All the bullets flying overhead didn't faze me really, just what would happen if I got hit.
>
> The Army got the worst of it that day and we had it easy in comparison to the taking of one of the bunkers on the beach head that would serve as our base of operations. The Army still kept moving forward off the beach and enabled us to set up all our gear when we were ordered to. *(Shipmate Charles W. Arcieri Brings Bunker Online*—(Summarized by SGT Kenneth Hall)

Carl Cannon of the 4th Infantry Division gives a close up view of Medal of Honor recipient Brigadier General Theodore Roosevelt, Jr., walking the beaches and making on the spot decisions, leading by example and undeterred by the fire. His account shows that while people may have found a way to contain their fear, "anyone who tells you they weren't afraid is either a damn fool or a damn liar." Cannon's account is especially noteworthy in the way it captures General Roosevelt's words at Utah Beach.

> I was still in the 4th Infantry Division on D-Day at Utah Beach. The landing was south and the stiff winds and the high waves pushed us 1000 yards too far south. We knew from the briefings how our landing looked. General Roosevelt came in and the first thing he said was "This is the wrong place."

> General Roosevelt talked to Colonel Johnson and Colonel Howell and suggested we withdraw, reload, and try and get to our designated landing point. Well, we ended up making our way in right where we landed. General Roosevelt had a walking stick in his right hand, and a .45 pistol in his left. He was directing all of us to get in to Sainte-Mère-Église [Author's Note: Sainte-Marie-du-Mont] and we all thought he was the best.

> If anyone tells you they weren't afraid, they were a damn liar or a damn fool. When we hit the beach with machine gun nests, pillboxes, and artillery facing us, and soldiers all around us were getting blown in half with body parts landing in the foxholes we took up positions in, we were all terrified.

> The engineers removed 15,000 mines off the beach. Someone set off a "Bouncing Betty" mine and if you were within 15 or 20 yards of that explosion, you weren't coming back.

> Another thing we had to face was flooded swamp land on the other side of the dunes, between us and Puckaville (Author's Note: Turqueville). The Germans had flooded a lot of places to about waist deep or six feet in places. A lot of paratroopers drowned in those areas because of their chutes and equipment and it's too hard to swim with all that weight on you. (*4th ID's Carl Cannon Faces the Visible Enemy Head-On*—(Summarized by SGT Kenneth Hall)

Walter Condon was up and packed early on the 4th of June, 1944. He and his fellow infantry men from the 29th ID were loaded down with 72 pounds of gear and ammunition, plus two days worth of food rations, and a single canteen of water. Equipped with an inflatable life preserver, that often left its users floating upside down in the water, he and the others disembarked from England on an LCT carrying a bulldozer and one thousand pounds of dynamite to be used for clearing obstacles on the Normandy beachhead. But for Condon and the others, it was the typical "hurry up and wait" that soldiers of every war had had to encounter.

It was four in the morning when we finally got the message the invasion was delayed. On the second day, there was no place on the LCT to sit down. After two days of standing up on the LCT, we finally got in to Normandy two miles off the mark we were supposed to land on at Omaha Beach. All we thought about was our mission. We should have gone straight in, but we were too tired to worry about it. We were about the first vehicle to get off the beach to the D-1 transit area. We went on to St Lo from there. We dug a good trench so the cows or enemy soldiers couldn't get over. (*29th ID's Walter Condon Stood Fast on the Brink of Infamy*—(Summarized by SGT Kenneth Hall)

**Allied soldiers on an American transport crossing the
English Channel wait to disembark onto the beaches of Normandy.**
(http://docs.fdrlibrary.marist.edu)

VI. Scaling the cliffs with the Rangers

The cliffs in the vicinity of Omaha Beach were one of the key early invasion targets. It was critical to the success of the mission for the large gun emplacements along the heights to be neutralized, as they were directly set to stop any entry from Omaha beach. Former Company Commander Ralph Goranson of 2nd Ranger Battalion, Company C, led his men in the attack on this important beach flank. Others went up Pointe du Hoc to knock the guns out of commission at that location. Both sets of men going up the cliffs were Rangers. They were an elite group of men that had been trained for this very purpose, and much more. Months of training in all types of terrain had made these men capable of thinking on their own and exercising initiative without delay. Their ability to make decisions quickly and soundly had been honed through the most rigorous training the Army had to offer. Sixty years later, Ralph Goranson gave his account of what it was like to lead his Rangers up the cliffs of Normandy. He was a twenty-two year old Company Commander leading men in combat. There was no doubt in his mind about the task before him. He recalled this exchange between his brother, who also was in the invasion, and himself, "'One thing I want you all to do: The minute you get out of that boat, if you get a shot, kick ass!' So we knew what we had to do."

Goranson's mission was to secure the right flank of Omaha Beach. He and his men had two hundred feet of sand to cross before scaling cliffs of fifty to seventy-five feet in an area that in Goranson's words was "littered with machine gun nests and dugouts." Goranson gives details of his company's heroic ascent and subsequent encounters with the German defenders.

> Oh, they were worried when we went in. And when we went there, there weren't many left. I mean we had gotten in there but . . . we knew it would be fortified and it was. There were a lot of honeycombs . . . .

> I was in a right flank boat and my boat was destroyed . . . Everybody got off but the boat was destroyed and the crew got on another boat . . . What happened immediately was machine gun fire all over the place. And my instructions were you know: The rest is going to be fine. Get your fanny across the beach and get in a firing position and then go about our missions. And our mission was to clear the right flank of the beach but unfortunately, I lost thirty-five men out of seventy—almost eighty, before they got out of the boat.

> We knew where we were going and the area that we wanted to tree climb was too high and there was a bunch of wire around and in the middle these old, weathered signs—*achtung minen* you know. I looked at it and I said "bullshit." . . . It wasn't mines. So we went up and right over into the country . . . over here. This is where the only paved roads came down to the beach and then the road went east . . . I tell you we had a cliff

that was about fifty to seventy feet and it wasn't the easiest to get over . . . I took a couple guys and I said go. And they went into the barbwire and they cut it and . . . they got up there and . . . well once they got up there, here was a trench system. It led every which way and there were very few people left, but over here was the box. This great big bunker . . . and the bullets and the bodies and everything all piled up . . . we had C-4[6] . . . then when the door went we put in one of those nice grenades that do a lot of burning—I don't know what you call it . . . incendiary, and then moved on. But they were crawling back . . . along the shore that connected to the highway, which I think the villagers called Hotel Samira, and that's where the German headquarters were . . . It was a mess . . . quite a few gave up. I think they could see the handwriting on the wall . . . you could see it was hidden and heavily fortified.

The idea was to protect that road that had been left open because . . . it ran all the way to where the others were coming from. (Ralph Goranson, 2nd Battalion Rangers, Commander of Company C—(Interview conducted by 49th MHD, transcribed by Lisa A. Zafirov)

VII. Moving inland

Once the gliders landed, and the planes and ships had discharged their passengers onto the beaches, marshes, and fields of Normandy, the real work began. It did not take long after the initial surprise attacks at places like Pegasus Bridge and Sainte-Mère-Église for word to get out that the long expected Allied invasion was occurring. There was no doubt in the minds of the Germans who were on the beaches of Normandy or in the towns along the Channel; but, still, it would be days before the German High Command in Berlin would approve the commitment of more forces and reserves. Worse still for the Germans, Field Marshall

---

[6]   C4 was not used in World War II. Its forerunner was called Nobel 808, and was typically used for missions described by Goranson.

Rommel was away. The American and British forces commanders were being led by men empowered to make decisions at the center of gravity of the fight, rather than from the vantage point of a table map. Ultimately, this costly delay would hurt the Germans and set the stage for a complete collapse of the lines (Stokesbury, 1980).

Sainte-Marie-du-Mont saw heavy fighting as Airborne troops landed around the village. At the cliffs and bluffs overlooking the channel, Rangers climbed up to surprise defenders in the heavy gun emplacements that were guarding the beach entry points.

Morning saw masses of American troops coming ashore at Utah and Omaha beaches, as well as a larger combined force of British and Canadian troops at Gold, Juno, and Sword Beaches. Wave after wave of troops came forward. They started to move inland. Airborne troopers scattered across the Norman landscape started to re-group and make their way to rally points. The next evening saw more troops flown over, even as bitter fighting continued along many of the beach villages. Within days, a long line of sustaining operations and logistical support started to emerge from the thousands of sea transport craft that lay in the channel between England and France. Instead of simply infantry men coming ashore, new specialties were arriving including special intelligence units and other units designed to go into the French interior and link up with allied French resistance or gather information from prisoners. The fighting would spread its way across a huge swath of villages and eventually turn into a field by field battle through the hedgerows dotting the Normandy countryside. A wearing down process started to occur, but the Germans were far from being beaten, and the Battle for Normandy was far from being won.

The accounts in this section include parts of the initial beach fighting and landings. They also provide other details of the fighting and experiences beyond the initial contact and days of the invasion. S.M. Harris was an intelligence officer for the Allies who landed early on D-Day. He was in the 1st Engineer Special Brigade. He was with a group known as "T" force. This team searched for people or documents that would give more information about the current situation of the German forces, and he was able to take a German official with top secret documents as his prisoner. Harris was responsible for six men. They came into the far end of Utah beach, an area known as Red Beach. Gathering his men together in all of the chaos while being shot at was a challenge.

Harris noted, "I was scared to death and very nervous . . . At times, we were a little lost, were being shot at, but not too bad off because we were focused on the job we had to do."

Once ashore, the men headed toward the U.S. First Army Headquarters. Harris reported with a pass granting him full access across the entire area of operations. It stated "This officer is to be given any aid he requires, and is free to go where and do what he wanted." Armed with this pass, Harris and his men scoured the Normandy countryside and soon had a number of prisoners.

> Our 'un-disclosed' mission was to look for places or people that might have intelligence, then seize and guard them. In North Africa, a lot of good intelligence was lost because troops didn't know what they had. We did our best to keep everyone informed as to what was valuable, assist in forwarding that information, and try and not get killed in the process. We were composed of different teams to seize enemy soldiers, operatives and their safe-houses.

> We had some prisoners for awhile—about six or seven. They were really happy to be taken prisoner. They were not the hard-core fighting types.

Harris made his biggest contribution when he captured a German in civilian clothes carrying vital information, about 100 miles from Paris.

> My coup of the war was when my driver and I stopped this German in civilian clothes, asking for ID. He said "I have many things that will be of interest to you." . . . The German had left his command, taking top secret stuff with him and was ready to turn it over to the Allies, and happily be taken prisoner in the process. As a result, I got a trip to London. Later on, this German defector had turned into quite a useful guy. (*S.M. Harris Was Finding Enemy Secrets*—(Summarized by SGT Kenneth Hall)

Shirley Hartline was one of the original members of the 82d Airborne Division and survived every campaign it fought in World War II. He was a Private first Class in G Company, 325th Glider Infantry. His company was committed on D+1, after the initial forces had already encountered stiff resistance and heavy losses. He recalls that June 7, 1944, a rainy day, was the coldest day of his life. They were attacked the day after their glider landed in Normandy. The heavy fighting that followed did not leave him unscathed. He spent 31 consecutive days in combat, was wounded, and later returned to his unit for another operation in Holland.

> After 31 consecutive days of combat, without any replacements, we had one officer and five enlisted men left in G Company of the 325th Glider Infantry. I did not return unscathed from that operation as I was wounded during that time. The injury did not prevent me from rejoining what was left of my company, and jumping into Holland with the rest of the 82nd during Operation Market Garden. *(82nd's Shirley R. Hartline Returns from Normandy Abyss*—(Summarized by SGT Kenneth Hall)

John Johnson arrived into the fighting on D+4. He spent a month under fire and then was wounded and sent back for medical treatment. He recalls D+6, when he was surrounded by a beach filled with bodies of both Allied and German dead, as well as animals caught in the cross fire. Overhead, rounds from naval guns in the channel firing at the enemy were exploding, both on the land and in the air. He and his men moved in quickly and were immediately in the action.

> We went in pretty quick and the crews that I was with started clearing villages and taking friendlies back to the beach, they had a compound, until they started putting soldiers into the 4th and 90th Infantry Divisions.
>
> I don't know the name of the town, but it wasn't very far in . . . it was very active . . . I was wounded on the sixth of July and I left the 90th [Division] then. I was going to stabilize in a field hospital . . . . around an area known as L122. (John Johnson,

Private, Grenadier in the 9th Infantry Division—(Interviewer: J. Patrick Hughes, V Corps Command Historian, transcribed by Erin Livingston)

VIII. One German soldier's account

Joseph Horn was a German soldier who survived D-Day. He was on his dinner break when the first Allied paratroopers started to land near his post. His account shares some of the same perspectives of the Allied soldiers of the time. Horn was German, but he shares a common bond found in the descriptions of all soldiers fighting for their country, Axis or Allied. His account and background is not so different from many of the American World War II vets. Born in 1925, he was drafted into the military in 1943 and saw. combat in Africa prior to being assigned to Normandy. We find in Joseph Horn not a German Nazi, but a young man who was caught up in the middle of the same struggles as his peers on the battlefield, far from the politics but in the middle of the fighting. He was trained as a telegraph operator, sending Morse code messages for an artillery unit providing fire support to the Division stationed at Carentan. His position on D-Day was one kilometer behind Sainte-Marie-du-Mont. Horn recalls the 6th of June, 1944.

> I had been given the order to look after the telephone wire. Three hours northern direction and three hours back all the way testing the telephone wires and back at 9 o'clock in the afternoon (evening). And I was told I could eat something and make telephone service from 10 pm until midnight. Shortly after midnight you could hear very low flying American airplanes, 100 or 200 meters high and you could see parachuters jumping. Parachuters had ammunition and food and camouflage . . . This area was not under water but most of the area around Carentan was flooded. (Herr Joseph Horn, German Army—Interview by Dr. J. Patrick Hughes, 3 June 2004. Transcribed by Julie Heacock)

IX. The liberated

The purpose of the Invasion was to liberate the people of mainland Europe from their Nazi occupiers. Two accounts from D-Day 60 provide a glimpse into the vantage points of the occupied people. Alfred Fauvel was a ten-year-old boy during the Nazi Occupation of France. He tells of his experiences of helping Allied prisoners escape with the help of the French Underground.

Fauvel's family took in a Canadian and an American soldier, provided them with clothes, and worked with the resistance in assisting them to get back to the allied lines. On another occasion, seven soldiers escaped from where they were being held by the Germans. One of his neighbors, Monsieur Ourela, took the Americans and hid them in different villages, two at a time moving them day or night, whenever German eyes were not looking. Fauvel gives details about how such escapes were conducted.

> Our village was surrounded by Germans. We gave them civilian clothes so they would look like us. One of the American prisoners would not take off his combat boots. He had a tattoo on his forearm of the American flag. He'd roll his sleeve up and we would keep telling him to keep his sleeves down. A member of the French Resistance Movement came and took them to the fisherman. From there, they went out to sea where they would join up with an American ship. *(Going Underground: Young French Boy helps Allies Escape Prison Camp*—(Summarized by SGT Kenneth Hall)

Pierre Collard was a member of the Maquis, [7] the French Underground who was disappointed that the French government would

---

[7] Collard was in his 90's at the time of his interview. He may have mixed up some of his facts here. Technically the Maquis was a separate part of the French Resistance movement, just like the communists and other organizations. There were multiple sources of command and direction. He also said he was in the FFI, the Maquis, and the U.S. 2nd INF DIV. He may have changed units or his organization may have changed. Additionally, the interpreter himself may not have fully translated or understood the

not let him and the other veterans do a jump into Normandy. Collard was a member of the French battalion of the U.S. 2nd U. S. Infantry Division during the time of the invasion. The activities of the Maquis forced the Germans to obligate or deploy forces throughout the invasion. According to Collard, General Eisenhower said that the work of the Maquis Resistance was the equivalent of 15 Divisions.[8] Collard describes the resistance activities conducted by his organization to an interviewer, who had the help of a translator. All the men in his unit were former French soldiers. Though the Germans disbanded the army, these men and others decided to continue the fight against the occupier. Armed with a variety of weapons such as an English STEN Gun (submachine gun), M1 Carbine, no anti-tank weapons and little else, Collard and his fellow resistance fighters sabotaged "trains, roads, bridges . . ." and conducted ambushes. Collard and his comrades received orders from London via radio and worked with Allied agents who helped them plan and coordinate their activities.

> They had . . . an American officer helping direct the Maquis. And they also had two British officers and an Irish woman who also worked with them . . . at the time when he participated in the Maquis, he was in his twenties. He said . . . that his unit was a regular army unit (FFI) *Forces Francais de Interieur*. It was one company.

Collard goes on to describe the actions of his unit during the time of the invasion at Normandy.

> They say the first big prefecture was liberated in Bayeux by the British, but that is not true, because we liberated the first office in . . . a prefecture in La Creuse. [La Creuse was in Central France where the Maquis Operated. According to

difference between the units as he provided the translation. Collard's report still offers tremendous insight into the spirit and leadership of a man who fought in the long struggle to liberate his country.

8   General Eisenhower, in his book, *My Crusade in Europe (1948)* wrote that the work of the Maquis was equivalent to fifteen divisions

Zabecki (1999) there were several resistance groups, but the Maquis were not active in the Normandy area. Nevertheless, Collard was involved in operations against the German forces at the time of Operation Overlord.] We only kept the city for two days. It was hard to defend against a German unit that came from southern France, from Toulouse. It was an SS division and they were responsible for a horrible massacre, burning women and children in a church. But we held them off for eight days, ambush after ambush on their way out. They were on their way to Normandy, this SS unit, but they arrived twelve or thirteen days late, and by then, we had established a good foothold . . . (Interview with Pierre Collard translated by LTC Millett for LTC Alan R. Koenig.)

Even in this short review of the various battlefield scenes, we get a clear sense that there were countless instances where different leadership styles and skills came into play. Every situation differed, and every decision was based on the factors and environment in which the individual was placed.

Together, these men, and all of the others fighting at Normandy were part of a greater effort that slowly, but thoroughly, chipped away at and eventually broke through the wall that kept the Allies out of Hitler's Fortress Europe. Many of them never made it beyond the beaches of Omaha or Utah, or past their drop zones around Sainte-Mère-Église and Sainte-Marie-du-Mont. Some men were captured, others fought all the way through to the end of the war and saw its worst atrocities.

The accounts described leadership experienced from the lowest level—such as between two comrades of equal rank—to the first line squad leaders and NCOs leading the way, and on up to the level of the officers leading platoons and companies. They presented a commentary on organizational level leadership as well, such as that described in the Slapton Sands incident by Harold McCauley.

Ultimately, it comes down to cause and effect. The situation, the environment, and the mission all made up the causes for the actions that were taken by leaders, with the effect being the success or failure of a landing, a skirmish, a reconnaissance patrol, or even landing troops at the beaches or dropping them from the sky. This compelling sampling of accounts by the men who were there gives us the setting for the D-Day leadership laboratory that we will use to explore leadership theory. Though it in no way gives the whole picture of the battle, it provides a basis for understanding the nature of the chaotic experiences and challenges faced by the men we studied. We used these accounts and others to illustrate observations of leadership in action and how it affected personnel at all levels.

CHAPTER 4

FIRST LINE LEADERS:
COMPANY AND BELOW

THIS CHAPTER FOCUSES ON THE accounts of first line leaders: Men who literally were in the front, leading their troops and actively participating in formal leadership roles. The emergence of leadership in this group was noted in nearly every account. These aspects of first line leadership will involve the following areas:

> Composite picture: who were the first line leaders?
> Similarities of first line leaders
> Emerging leadership experiences
> Compassionate leadership
> Making use of rebel streaks among leaders

What sort of leadership was displayed at D-day among the first line of leaders, those who were on the ground directly impacting the motivation, mission objectives, and outcomes of the action? First line leaders were involved in each part of the operation, from the squad leader with only a few soldiers, to the platoon sergeant or young lieutenant, to captains who led companies of soldiers. All of them were at the nexus of the fighting—slogging ashore through the water, jumping out of the airplanes, landing in the gliders. They fought in the hedgerows and went house to house fighting the enemy. They used innovative techniques to overcome obstacles and "outside the box" thinking to win on the beach, in the hedgerow country, and on the hills overlooking the beach. Throughout the interviews, there were constant examples of this leader and what he did. The first line leader was not always the same, but there were many examples which suggest a composite picture of who that leader was and what made him that way.

Theoretical Perspectives on the First Line Leaders

Many of the First Line leadership observations from the study can be framed with leader-member exchange theory (LMX). This theory presents a structure for explaining the process that occurs between leaders and followers. It focuses on the interactions between the leader and the follower(s), with the key part of this being the dyadic relationship that occurs during the exchange.

In LMX theory, the leader and follower form a negotiated bond to determine what the specific roles and responsibilities will be. In the units at Normandy, there were several different layers of LMX that occurred at the squad, platoon, company, and battalion levels and higher. In LMX, there are vertical dyads formed between the leader and the followers. Those followers who conform to the leaders' standards and expectations form an in-group. Those followers who are not willing to meet these same standards and expectations comprise an out-group. According to this theory, a leader may treat all followers equally under the terms of a standard social contract. However, the followers who work into the in-group look for more innovative ways to accomplish the group mission. In this way, they accomplish more for the leader's goal, and the leader in turn reciprocates by spending more time and being more open to exchange of ideas with members of the in-group. The impact of this is substantial.

In the case of first line leadership, the process between building a larger in-group and reducing the out-group occurred early in the team building (training) process. The intense training, discipline and military structure, and the common need to come together as a functioning team helped facilitate this process and accelerated the change from out-groups to in-groups. LMX has three phases built on four factors (see Table 1). The leaders at D-Day had the challenge to develop a strong enough rapport with their men to get them from Phase 1, Stranger, to Phase 3, Partner in as little time as possible.

Table 1. The Three Phases of Leader Member Exchange Theory

	Phase 1 STRANGER	Phase 2 ACQUAINTANCE	Phase 3 PARTNER
Roles	Scripted	Tested	Negotiated
Influences	One Way	Mixed	Reciprocal
Exchanges	Low Quality	Medium Quality	High Quality
Interests	Self	Self/Other	Group

(From Northouse, 2004, originally published in "Relationship-based Approach to Leadership: Development of Leader-Member Exchange (LMX) Theory of Leadership Over 25 Years: Applying a Multi-level, Multi-Domain Perspective," by G.B. Graen and M. Uhl-Bien, 1995, *Leadership Quarterly*, 6(2), 231)

The first line leaders we studied demonstrated that under the circumstances at D-Day, they generally were able to reach Phase 3. The accounts show a genuine regard by soldiers for leaders, and vice versa. The examples of the leader dealing with conflict in the group and negotiating through the challenges and asserting his will are present as well. Lastly, the mutual willingness to sacrifice for the group shows that a tremendous amount of bonding occurred and emerged, even in cases where there was not a long period of time to develop this. However, because of the nature of the situation at D-Day and the great challenges and impending danger at that time, the emergence of leadership and followership traits appeared to be accelerated, especially when viewed in light of the accounts where spontaneous leadership and group formation occurred. In these cases, the normal thawing procedures and basic exchanges were rapid, with leadership changing out perhaps as often as every few hours or days, depending on the type of combat situation. This suggests that time may not be as great of a factor as the model suggests and lends weight to the idea that leadership traits will emerge under compressed events and circumstances.

A good example of this is when one goes on an airplane ride and strikes up a conversation with the passenger sitting in the next seat.

There is a slight tension from traveling in the air and the possibility of danger, as well as the fact that someone traveling alone may not feel as sure of oneself as in familiar surroundings. The result of this is often a very engaging and lively discussion that can make the trip go by faster. Though not everyone has such conversations, many of us do. This is one example of how human traits surface as a self-protective mechanism, a natural inclination to develop a group or ally to turn to in the event something unexpected occurs. At D-Day, this would have been a fairly common occurrence, especially among the paratroopers who were from different units as they were trying to re-group after being scattered across the Norman countryside. Basically, the in-group became any allied forces member, the out-group was also pushed to the extreme—anyone who was not an ally was a potential target. In this way, the men at Operation Overlord (D-Day) were fortunate. They knew who the enemy were and had clarity in who was friendly and who was not.

The framework of LMX is helpful to provide a way to describe the processes that went on between leaders and followers, in both formal and formal groups at D-Day. However, it should be noted that in order for the LMX to function it required a degree of competency in leadership traits to be present or to emerge from both the leader and follower.

Leadership Similarities among First Line Leaders

As discussed in the introduction, the first line leader was in the front leading his troops. Most of the men in this study were first line leaders at one time or another during their wartime service. The term "first line leader" will be broadly applied to those leaders who ranged in rank from Corporal through Captain. Normally, the first line leader is the first leader in an individual soldier's chain of command. But for the purposes of this study, we are broadening the range because there was so much interaction between such a wide range of ranks. The first line leader saw to the successful training of his troops. The 82d Airborne's Duke Boswell recalled that:

> We were staying in an airport hanger for a few days before
> D-Day, sitting around and getting exercise in now and then
> or play some cards. Then they told us where we were going.

> Each platoon was shown their objective. Then, the company commanders explained what was expected of us. We were very well-briefed with what was coming and what we had to do (Boswell).

Boswell was a member of an elite parachute unit that still has a renowned reputation for its *esprit de corps* and vigorous training. The leadership he saw displayed around him on a daily basis allowed him to have confidence in the men who led him, while at the same time gave him the same level of assurance for his soldiers. The training they received played an important role in this.

Another first line leader was Corporal Harry Browne. Browne was not in an elite unit, but he nonetheless observed solid leadership on many levels. He relates this anecdote about a former platoon leader:

> It was, the leadership you're talking about, yes it was good. We had a Lt. we called him the goon. I can see him today. He built about like you are, about your size, and had a mustache, big mustache, he walked kind of like an old farmer. Never in a hurry, nothing bothered him, and he was always right there when something was going on . . . He was just a, you just didn't get excited with him around. Guys figured they had a lot of confidence in him, and he knew what he was doing, and we trusted him. He proved to be very, very good, knowledgeable (Browne, H.).

Browne served in the 2nd Infantry Division and said that the leadership, "could not be any better" (Browne, H.). Thus, we have two first line leaders from different units who observed and expressed similar confidence in their leaders. This was a recurring theme in the study group.

29th Infantry Division's Walter Condon talked about his impression of the hastily trained new lieutenants that were on the battlefield at D-Day. Condon spoke of the "90 day wonders" [9] with these words,

---

9   The "90 day wonders" was the term applied to graduates of the Officer Candidate School Course that transitioned Enlisted and Non-commissioned Officers to 2nd Lieutenants in a much more rapid

In time of war, the most important man is a "90-day wonder." This would be a new lieutenant as the casualties were high in that group. They would come in every week or two. They had to look brave, act brave and lead the rest of us who were tired all the time over the hedgerows. There ought to be a special memorial for them (Condon).

5th Infantry Division's Peter Molinari also had positive words about his leaders, including the lieutenants:

I had a great deal of respect for my immediate officers. We had a couple of great lieutenants. We called one by his first name because he didn't want to be identified by the enemy during the battles (Molinari).

Henry French was a Sergeant in the 1st Infantry Division's 16th Infantry Regiment. He echoed the sentiments of the others in his description of not only one, but two commanders. His first Commander was Captain Joseph Dawson, who led him at Normandy. He states here:

F: But anyway we were the first ones to get on top of the hill. And (Inaudible) Captain Dawson said, "When the wind blow, let's go!" So . . .

I: Captain Dawson?

F: Yea.

I: Was he your Commander?

F: Yea. He was Company Commander. Joseph P. Dawson.

I: Joseph P. Dawson?

---

fashion than the traditional four year process to get commissioned such as through the Military Academy or Reserve Officer Training Corps.

F: Yea.

I: Was he a good guy?

F: Oh, he was excellent. He didn't say "Okay, you men go here, go there and do this". He said "C'mon, let's go!" He was out front. One hundred percent, all of him.

I: You'd probably follow him anywhere. (French)

French goes on to talk about his second Commander, CPT Crooks {Interviewer was unsure if it was Crooks or Crisp}:

F: Yes, he (Dawson) was wounded and then . . . they sent him back to the States. Captain Crooks take his place.

I: Was he a pretty good leader?

F: Oh yea. Crooks was a real good guy too. I met him.

I: Wow, you were blessed to have so many good officers!

F: Oh yea.

I: Usually they always tell us officers were not that good.

F: Oh, we had good, excellent, first class in my book.

F: Yes. Dawson, he found the trails. You know, the German's had their trails and he just helped me find one and there we went in (Inaudible) and knock out with a couple machine guns and rifle (French).

The fact that the interviewer expressed a level of surprise at French's description of his officers illustrates that some perceptions of officer leadership may need to be re-examined. In all of these descriptions, there is a level of fondness and confidence in the leader. The leader was a trainer and a participant. Leaders who led the way and shared in the perils of their soldiers were respected.

Perhaps the best example of what first line leadership at the company level could do is expressed in the words of Ralph Goranson, who was an OCS (Officer Candidate School) graduate at Normandy. Goranson was a Ranger who commanded a company on D-Day. Goranson went to Fort Benning to attend OCS, the same place that still graduates young lieutenants today from the ranks of enlisted soldiers. Goranson's recollection of how he ended up going to OCS is similar to how many others related their experiences. He had the combination of background and skills that were readily apparent to his leadership early on in his Army career:

> Because of my D.C. (Author's note: Drill Corps) training which {I} had in high school, and when I graduated there, I was set in command of the regiment. I found out much to my chagrin that I was classified as a cook. [laughs] But the Company Commander said, "Don't worry." He said, "We're promoting you as a supply sergeant. You will be the acting supply sergeant and go out on the firing range and things like that to qualify but in the meantime you're running the supply."
>
> So . . . on the day we were graduating, within one or two hours the old man was chewing me out because I didn't have my stripes on. [laughs]
>
> Well I'd say there {I} was a Supply Sergeant and he called me in once or twice about applying for officer school—OCS. And I said, "Well maybe . . ."
>
> So one time I had a two day leave and I went down to L.A. to get a friend of mine and I came back and there was Pappy—a First Sergeant with two million years in the service, waiting for me at the bus stop, "Get off! Get cleaned up! Get your ass over to the board!" [Laughs] So I did that and I was approved to go to Benning . . . We graduated more applicants from that group I think than from any group that went through there . . . we were as goofy as hell but we had a good group. (Goranson)

Goranson reveals much about his training and the character of those around him, as well as those above him in this passage. He was identified early on to have some important leadership skills, but then also proved to be capable in the duties assigned to him. Eventually, his leadership was recognized to the point that his leaders practically made him go to OCS. Once there, he found many others like himself who were all a cut above the rest, "goofy as hell, but we had a good group". Goranson graduated with one of the largest OCS classes at Fort Benning. His leadership was enhanced by his desire for more responsibility and challenges. His commanders saw this and not only encouraged him, but also rewarded his drive. Goranson describes the experience:

> G: Our class, I don't know who were the people but we graduated more . . .

> I: Students.

> G: [More students] at that time than had ever graduated . . . it was a fun bunch. I don't know what happened to any of the guys because I went off to the—I went out for infantry lieutenant, which I got sick and tired of and that's why I put in for Ranger School and I was taken in there. I went into the Ranger Regiment for a while that had a full eagle (Colonel) battalion commander {Interviewer comments: normally a Lieutenant Colonel leads a battalion.} . . . I applied for everything I could. Well I was training there and the Colonel, uh, Major then, called me into his office and said, "I'd like you to take over the Charlie Company as the Commanding Officer. He said, "Nope. No questions, no answers. You want the job or you don't want the job." He was a great big guy. I said, "Well I want the job." And he said, "Well you got the job. Well, what are you sitting there for? Go get that company in shape (Goranson).

Just the way that Goranson describes the vignette between himself and the Major who offers him the job shows the core of Goranson's drive. He made a decision, and he had no hesitation at that point to accept it. He displayed some of the requisite traits that a company commander must have—maturity, judgment, and decisiveness.

Goranson led a Ranger Company at D-Day on Omaha Beach. He lost 35 out of 70 men within minutes of escaping their sinking vessel as it pulled into shore. Throughout the event he maintained his bearing and his mission. Not every Commander or Officer at D-Day did this; but throughout the accounts in the study group these leaders managed to do this.

An 82d Airborne soldier, Curt Hatcher recalled how this happened during the parachute jump into Sainte-Mère-Église:

> When you're there, you don't know all the workings. You're really looking over your shoulder, and trying to protect yourself and get your job done. MAJ Krause[10] was good at getting all of us organized while we were still scattered all over the place. After we got control of the town, the Major had an American flag flown over the town hall building, which he carried since the units' actions in Naples, Italy (Hatcher).

Hatcher recalls Krause as a Major, the Regimental Executive Officer, but others recall him as a Colonel, the Brigade Commander. One referred to him as "Cannonball Krause" (Boswell; Delaney). Regardless of this difference in title, several soldiers recalled his actions and the flag he carried. And, regardless of his rank, because of the circumstances of the event he still was a direct leader on the ground with the men who landed. He immediately took charge, organized, and gave direction for the soldiers who soon started to form up and gather in groups.

The Airborne troops were scattered all over the Norman countryside according to the accounts in the study. Fifteen members of the Study Group were 82d Airborne veterans. Many others were from the 101st. These veterans were from units with high standards and demanded more from their soldiers than other units. People did not just become Airborne. They had to earn entry into the organization, and they had to meet higher standards. It is not exceptional that a Ranger or an Airborne

---

[10] As mentioned in the text there are several variations of the rank for Lieutenant Colonel Edward Krause, who was the Battalion Commander. Prior to this he was the Regimental XO (Executive Officer) as a Major. LTC Krause received the Distinguished Service Cross for his actions on 6-7 June 1944 at D-Day.

Paratrooper would carry the requisite traits needed for leadership after such a vetting process.

However, not all first line leaders at company level were in elite units. Nevertheless, their accounts are just as compelling, if not as exciting as jumping out of an airplane first. One of these leaders was Irv Koplovitz. He became a First Sergeant in a personnel company under these circumstances prior to D-Day. Nearly all of Koplovitz's squadron chain of command was killed in the flight from America to England when the transport carrying them to England was sunk by torpedo. However, Koplovitz and others in the unit rose to the challenge. Koplovitz describes how he and his troops felt about being dealt such a loss, even before going into combat:

> It was certainly the lowest morale point we had. We quickly rallied and reminded ourselves that we were trained to do a job and that we had to do that job no matter what happens. So, with each assignment we got, we carried it out to the fullest (Koplovitz).

Koplovitz' account was consistent with the accounts of many other first line leaders. They did not need Airborne Wings or a Ranger patch[11] to demonstrate their leadership. They did what they had to do when called upon to do so.

One of these, William McNamara, was a military journalist. He led six men ashore at Omaha and on through Europe, recording events of the War. McNamara was an officer in charge of a group of men who covered the news of troop movements and personnel experiences. His office was on a ship off of Omaha Beach until they came ashore with a radio and mimeograph machine in his jeep (McNamara).

McNamara may not have been the "tough" leader seen in other units, but his contributions and those of his men in recording the history of D-Day and the rest of the War were nonetheless critical, longstanding contributions.

---

[11] During World War II, the Ranger patch was a blue lengthwise diamond with the word Ranger embroidered in yellow.

Others had less formal entry into leadership roles. Francis Lamoureux of the 508th PIR (Parachute Infantry Regiment), 82d Airborne became a leader simply by being a volunteer:

> So when I hear the word volunteer my ears perk up, so I went to Captain Bogath who was the commanding officer of our G Company. I asked Captain Bogath I hear rumors that they need men for this special mission they've got going around for the invasion. So I'd like to volunteer for it. I did the same thing at Aberdeen, when I was there I went to the company commander and there's a notice on the bulletin board that they're looking for volunteers for the airborne. I told them, hey, sign me up, I volunteer. He said, "Lamoureux are you crazy? You want to be a paratrooper?" I said. "sign me up." They put me in charge of a detail, at that time they still considered me a regular Army, so by serial number 0011888-0 became all but 3's with the draftees. So I got put in charge of that detail and only five of us volunteered for that detail and we took the training down. I just herd them—shepherd them down to Ft. Benning to get the jump schooling in. So that was the first time I got put in charge of a detail of men, where I had to take care of those guys. I was responsible for getting them there, and at that time I was only a Private (Lamoureux).

Lamoureux's spirit of volunteerism and desire for responsibility led him to be identified as a soldier who could be counted to take action when others were not watching. He was a self-starter. His initiative led him to levels of responsibility others would never have.

Many of the jobs did not involve fighting the enemy directly. Many of the heroes of D-Day had to fulfill gruesome tasks that others would not have been capable of doing, such as recovering bodies. Samuel Lence of the 79th Infantry Division was one such leader. Lence not only had a tough job, but also had to take care of his men. It put him at odds with others at times and resulted in him losing rank three times. Lence felt he had to take up for his men even if it meant getting in trouble. He recalls the challenges that came with his job:

One of my primary jobs was retrieving bodies from the landing craft, and bodies hung up on the pylons, and bodies ensconced in the propellers of the landing craft—Higgins boats, you name it. I had to dive for some of them, but I couldn't dive deep enough without equipment.

I: You were busted down (in rank)? You were a sergeant three times?

L: I was a son-of-a-bitch. My last break was on account of a fist fight with a mess sergeant. He wouldn't feed our crew because our charge-of-quarters failed to wake us up (Lence).

This small piece from Lence's account shows the human tragedy of the fight. Throughout his account, he refers to the waste of it all. Certainly, someone who had this task had an eyewitness view of the carnage of war. Yet, he stuck to his mission and took care of his men. The fist fight with the Mess Sergeant is a classic tale of the GI out in the field coming in to the confines of some camp, only to be told he is too late for chow. As the leader, Lence takes on the bureaucracy (in this case the Mess Sergeant), because rules or no rules, his men need to eat. He may have lost rank, but he certainly maintained the loyalty of his men by his actions, and he later earned his rank back. Lence was not unique as a rebellious first line leader. There were others in the group that had to use unconventional methods to accomplish the mission. Harold McCauley broke the nose of one of his soldiers to get him to be a team player. In today's environment and its revised standards of leadership and conduct, this would be a problem, but when you are preparing for a critical event like D-Day, some of the civilities can be lost:

I was in charge of three DUKWs. One guy had been in the engineers, and had been in every outfit in the Army. He ended up in our outfit because there was only one place worst than our unit, and that was the gliders. If we could not handle them they went to the gliders. We got into a fight. I was his corporal and he said something to me. I broke his nose. He broke my nose. Somehow, we ended up the best buddies that ever was. We got together at the reunions and cried every time (McCauley).

The fact that McCauley had to show the guy who was boss eliminated friction in the relationship. McCauley acted in a consistent manner and fixed the problem, earned the man's respect, and eventually they both benefited from a better relationship and performance because they were able to form a cohesive team with clear lines drawn.

Many first line leaders did not have time to mince words or sugarcoat things. There was a war going on around them. When they encountered resistance that did not pass the common sense test, they dealt with it, regardless of the consequences they might face afterwards. This was a trait that many of them had to have in order to survive. Staff Sergeant Paul Merriman of the 736th Field Artillery Battalion witnessed an incredible series of events, reacted to them, and then went on to rejoin his unit, all in one night. His unit Commander and First Sergeant were in a convoy of vehicles that blew up, killing several people including the Commander. Merriman was the driver in a second vehicle because another driver had poor night vision. The lead vehicle hit a land mine, blowing the vehicle in to the air. Merriman describes the scene and his actions that saved the lives of several people:

> First thing we did was check out our people. Their right legs in most cases were like mush . . . I took a knife and sliced part of the boot off of them, slit the bottom of their trousers, and as carefully as I could put some sulfa powder into the wounds, covered parts of the legs that were hurt, and we administered sulfa pills to those who were wounded to prevent infection. Then the medics came in, but there was only one. We rode with them, and Captain Blum took them to the rear echelon for their first treatment. I stayed with them until about one or two o'clock as I recall and then I got a vehicle and caught up with my outfit (Merriman).

The way he recalls the event and the steps he took when it occurred show that Merriman could handle pressure, danger, and think at the same time. Despite the chaos of the landmine explosion, Merriman matter-of-factly recalls what they did.

Merriman also noted that the first line leaders were often killed because they were leading their troops in dangerous areas. This is a statement of the obvious, but his point was that it forced younger, inexperienced soldiers to have to take on roles and responsibilities they may not have been ready for, and as Merriman said, "they had to grow up fast":

> In the infantry, the officers and men go first. Unfortunately, this leaves things in a pretty bad state as we know from the stories of things that happened at D-Day. When you lose all your officers and sergeants on down, because they follow, it is pretty hard to get organized and keep things going; that's the tough part. You can't expect a man who is a corporal or even a private; he grows up in a big hurry. That was the unfortunate part of all that. In our case, (inaudible) we saw what was happening to these guys on point. It was always a sergeant or a corporal who would go out on point because somebody had to be in charge, the guy with the stripes (Merriman).

Eventually, Merriman, though only a Staff Sergeant, ended up commanding the battery he was in at one point, for a brief time at least, due to loss of the commander and other leaders.

Norman Schein was a member of the 248th Engineer Battalion. He was a sergeant who was resilient and smart. He knew how and when to act—and he saved lives because of it. Here is one example from his account in how he saved a fellow soldier after the jeep they were riding in was hit by enemy fire:

> The jeep was hit so I ran. Then I got up when they went for more ammo, and I had a .45 caliber submachine gun, which wasn't good for more than fifty yards, but it made a lot of noise, and I cut loose about sixty rounds at them, and they took off. He was hurt so bad, and we carried sulfa in bags on our belts, and I cut his pants off and put sulfa on one side and the other pack on the other side. I put a tourniquet on his leg. I didn't know exactly how I was going to get him out of there, but right behind those two French women . . . laying there all shot up, were some fence posts. I took his pants off and made strips out of them, and I tied them to the fence posts. I grabbed him by the collar and . . . got him to the jeep, which was still running. I . . . beat it back about nine miles to our

lines. They were just putting up a field hospital and they came running with their IVs and blood and they took his dog tags. They never took him off the jeep . . . He lost a lot of blood. Then they took him inside. The doctor was there, and I said, "Can I see him?" He said, "I want to talk to you about this." They stabilized him and put him in a wire basket. They said, "We can't do much for this man except get him blood and stabilize him." After they got him stabilized, he wanted his coat, so I went back to the jeep and got his coat, and it was full of shrapnel holes. I said, "You don't want this anymore do you?" He said, "I want it more than ever." So I put that beat-up old coat over him, and that's the last time I saw him. He wrote me several times. The doctor came up to me and he said, "Are you responsible for this?" I said "Yes sir." He gave me a hug and he said. "You just saved a man's life." If you hadn't gotten him here right away, he would have died. I was proud about that. He and I went through a lot. We got shot at. We got howitzers (shells fired) on us. I was wounded three times, and he got it once real bad. But we went through it. We made it (Schein).

Walter Raymond was another leader from the 79th ID. He was a corporal whose job was to look after his soldiers—both on the job and off the job. In one instance Raymond describes trying to keep his guys out of trouble and having to answer to "the old man" or CO (Commanding Officer):

> I would have still done the same thing. Cause even when we went out . . . I know like when we was just training they'd get—these guys would get drunk and stuff. I never drank. I used to get them back and every time they got busted I got busted. Captain would say, "Walter!" And I'd say, "Captain they're my guys and I got to take care of them." So . . . ok" (Raymond).

In another passage, Raymond describes the chaos at the landing and how he urged his troops to move out, as well as his motivation as the first man out of the ramp:

R: . . . . I just wanted to get out of this thing and get on land. That's what I wanted to do. I said, "If I'm going to go, I want to go on land. I don't want to go in the water." As soon as that thing was down I went.

I: When you were at the beach, and obviously there's a lot going on, did you have an initial impression? Or what were your actions?

R: No. It just . . . the thing was to work your way in. Get in after the Germans and just work your way in. Work your way in. Get away from the beach. Cause at the beach they were sawing everything up. You had to get away from the beach.

I: When did you finally feel safe?

R: When we were in about a mile or so, and it was rough but you know, what the hell and everything. A lot of guys were lost and different ones were out-of-it and everything.

I: . . . how many of your guys did you have with you when you felt safe a mile in?

R: Well I had about seven guys, seven or eight guys, and the guys were—going.

I: You just kept your squad together?

R: You kept your squad together and tried to keep contact with the rest of the company. That was the idea. You don't want to lose everybody (Raymond).

Walter Raymond never made it past Corporal. But to the six to twelve men he was responsible for during the war, it did not matter. What mattered was that he was conscientious and watched out for his men. Raymond noted that even a good leader cannot fix what is broken sometimes. He also discussed soldiers who went berserk and who could not be settled down:

I: Any instances of true leadership or cowardice for that matter coming up on that first day?

R: Oh we had guys that would go a little berserk and you'd see them, and then you wouldn't see them. I've seen guys.

I: What is the leadership response to that if you have a guy?

R: Well, you try and calm him down but you can't jeopardize a whole squad. More or less . . . he's on his own.

I: What does that mean go berserk? What do you mean by that?

R: Well you just . . . everything gets to him with the fighting and the killing and everything and that was it. You didn't . . . you just didn't care about anything anymore. You'd try and get a medic to get him and maybe give him a shot to calm him down or something, but you didn't (pause). Your time was . . . like I said everything moves so fast, that you just don't have time to tinker with. You try to do the best you can. That's it (Raymond).

Raymond, though only a Corporal at the time, had to deal with highly complex challenges in a compressed, quick timeline. "Everything moves so fast, you just don't have time to tinker with {it}." To survive the landing, get off the beach, move inland and engage the enemy every step of the way required skills and abilities that were either there or were not. Fortunately for Raymond's men, he had those skills. Raymond may not have realized the impact of his leadership, but the fact that he survived as a leader, shows that he was more than adequate for the job.

Like many other first line leaders, Raymond was wounded on more than one occasion. Yet despite that, all he could think of was to get back with his squad. Though this is related to the team bonding and the need to share in the group, it also speaks of his own internal traits as a leader to want to be there with his men:

I wanted to get well. I wanted to get myself well enough because I didn't want to be in there. I know the guys were out there and my outfit was there, and I just really wanted to go back, which I did. I got wounded like two or three times (Raymond).

It also was not uncommon for people to refuse care if it meant leaving their comrades. Though not a first line leader, one battalion commander kept going:

> Our 2nd battalion commander, Colonel Vandaborg (Author's note: Lieutenant Colonel Benjamin H. Vandervoort was commander of the 2nd Battalion, 505th PIR [Parachute Infantry Regiment]) fractured his ankle and we put a gas mask around it to protect it. He stayed with us right until then end, and even when they tried to evacuate him he refused (Delaney).

Similarly, 2nd Lieutenant John F. Kennedy of Company K, 13th Infantry Regiment was wounded three times but still managed to get back to his platoon to be with his men (Kennedy). The bonding, the training, and the sense of caring for one's men seem to have all played a significant role in many of these veteran's actions and inspired them to overcome wounds in order to carry out their duties and to keep going when they might have opted out of their leadership roles once they had been wounded. It seems rather more likely that the wounding created greater resolve and determination in them, and added to their sense of resolute purpose to "keep going."

Lt. John Landis of the 47th Infantry Regiment, 9th Infantry Division, took over command of his Company when the Commander was killed. His recollection of the American bombing at St. Lo, an event which cost hundreds of American lives demonstrates how this sense of duty and responsibility played out:

> One of the main things I remember was when one of our own airplanes bombed us and killed six hundred of our men. I know it was unintentional, but we were trying to break out of the hedgerows and they pulled us back about a mile. At that time the 1800 bombers came over and started dropping bombs on the German lines. The wind blew the smoke

back on us and the bombers behind them started dropping bombs on us and killed General McNair (Lieutenant General Leslie McNair) and I believe a Colonel from the Air Force who was in communications with the bombers. So they lost communications with them, and the following bombers had no idea of who they were bombing. They were just dropping bombs on the smoke and dust. Finally, somehow in about an hour they got it stopped. The men of course were wounded—a lot of them. The bombs had disoriented a lot of them so I just grabbed what men I could get a hold of and we had to advance. We got to our old position and I got about a hundred yards past that and I got hit with an airburst so . . . . that's when I left the Company (Landis).

This passage is in line with historic accounts, such as those provided by other men and by historians such as Stephen Ambrose. The St. Lo bombing was a devastating event. Allied forces were trying to break through the German's defensive lines. The plan was to soften the resistance by heavy bombing followed by a general attack by the Allies. Unfortunately, a heavy amount of smoke started drifting back into the American lines, even though they had pulled back to what was considered a safe distance. The poor communications of the time, compounded by the drifting smoke, resulted in heavy American casualties. To move oneself out of the bomb-induced stupor and to urge on fellow soldiers, was a major act of bravery and leadership.

The occurrence of sergeants and lieutenants taking on additional responsibilities and successfully leading their men is interesting to note. According to *Studies in Social Psychology in World War II* (Stouffer et al., 1949), there was significant disparity in the educational levels of officers, non-commissioned officers and enlisted men. By late 1944, the OCS program had churned out many thousands of officers, and the ranks of the Army were burgeoning with newly-commissioned lieutenants. These men were selected from the enlisted and non-commissioned officer ranks. Many were veterans and had several years of experience prior to being commissioned; others were more mature or had been educated prior to enlisting. They represented a broad swath of Americans from all economic and social levels. Many officers at D-Day had the same grit, determination, and discipline to do the hard jobs on the ground as the NCO's whom they led. Thomas Alley commented:

> We had excellent officers and commanders. They were hard as nails but great people to us. I had six different company commanders during the war. We lost them to wounds from the actions we lived through (Alley).

Likewise, the 82d's Ed Asbury said this of his commanders:

> Through the entire war, my chain of command was great, and we got great training. We all did what we were trained to do (Asbury).

Fellow 82nd Airborne member SGT Zane Schlemmer recalled his fellow soldiers and commanders with this observation:

> From officer to private, we all jumped from the same planes. If there were any misfits, they left very soon. Some people said we were like a pack of jackals, but I thought we were more like mongooses. Our officers were superb (Schlemmer).

This willingness to share in the hardships of the men was not without some humorous moments, even at the scariest of times. Faced with a grounded vessel at Normandy British Naval Lieutenant Michael D'Alton recounted this event:

> So we, on our own, went pottering along the beach, looking for any sort of gap to get into . . . quite a distance from where we first anchored . . . we grounded, he then ordered the door lowered, and I, as junior officer, was in charge of the lowering of the door for it. The door went down, but didn't appear to go the full way down. I thought that's curious. So we wound it up again . . . There was immense resistance. And the hands were toy, toiling as hard as they could on the handles. And as I say, commissioned or not, I lent a hand, too. And I wound as hard as any of them, until, suddenly, the two back buttons of my trousers burst. So every turn of the handle the door came up a

little more, my trousers went down a little more, too. Ultimately, with great effort, we got the door up to sea level (D'Alton).

Perhaps the greatest challenge was the heavy casualties, often in minutes due to bombs or heavy fire. The First Line leaders never really had the time to think about such things. They detached themselves from the events around them and kept going. Henry French, of G Co., 16th Infantry Regiment summed it up this way:

F: Oh yeah. There's bullets and (Inaudible) all around but one way to go. (Inaudible).

I: Just keep moving forward?

F: Keep moving forward then.

I: A lot of guys on your boat didn't make it?

F: Some didn't make it, yes. (Inaudible) (French).

This short exchange is stark in its presentation of what so many of these leaders ultimately had to carry with them from D-Day forward: the loss of the men they led. And, French's reply says it all in a quiet, dignified and respectful way, "Some didn't make it, yes." Whether one was Company Commander Frank Goranson, or SSG Merriman, desperately trying to save the lives of his own Commander, the weight of these losses was a tremendous challenge to deal with and still continue the journey. The weight of this responsibility and how these first line leaders handled it is explained in the next section.

Compassionate Leadership

Many of the soldiers who arrived on D-Day never made it past the beach, except when washed in by the waves. Others were fished out of the water by men like Samuel Lence. In the heat of battle, there was little time for men to pause and deal with their grief. Act now, grieve later was the mantra soldiers and leaders had to follow.

In the interview with SGT French, there is this exchange regarding the difficulties of dealing with the profound sense of loss one feels when comrades are lost in battle:

> I: Kind of messy isn't it?

> F: It is. You can't look back on those things. I don't.

> I: No.

> F: Just can't do it.

> I: No. And if you do, you can really make yourself pretty miserable if you dwell too long on those things (French).

For Lieutenant Landis, there was no time either:

> Well, I was an Executive Officer when I was assigned to the Company as a replacement officer and the Captain was killed and I took over command of the Company at the time" (Landis).

CPT Goranson also had no time to grieve during the fight, as he still had the other half of his troops to take care of. Goranson's account of scaling the ciffs and the loss of his men has already been presented, this critical part of his account is worth reviewing:

> G: Everybody got off but the boat was destroyed and the crew got on another boat. But the boat was [pause].

> I: So once those doors opened what happened immediately?

> G: What happened immediately was machine gun fire all over the place. And my instructions were you know: The rest is going to be fine. Get your fanny across the beach and get in a firing position and then go about our missions. And our mission was to clear the right flank of the beach but unfortunately, I lost thirty-five men out of seventy—almost eighty, before they got out of the boat.

Goranson lost 35 soldiers in a matter of minutes. Nevertheless, he and C Company still had a job to do. There was no time to pause for each soldier, or any opportunity to take a break until long after the men left behind had been collected for burial. Thus, there were no formal good-byes, merely a sudden break in a line or connection between different individuals who had collectively made up a team.

Corporal Howard Manoian of the 515th Parachute Infantry Regiment also had no choice but to keep going:

> Both my battalion commander and the executive officer were killed while we dropped from the heavens. Our 1st lieutenant then became battalion commander for awhile. A more senior officer was later brought in from the 508th and assumed that position (Manoian).

Leaders had to step up, take charge, and make decisions and they had no time to deal with the normal emotional challenges that accompany loss until much later. For Walter Raymond and his troops, it was constant motion:

> I: After a firefight, how long before your squad would calm down and the adrenaline slows down?
>
> R: Well we just kept moving, moving, moving you know. The only time your adrenaline went down was when there was nobody shooting back at you. Have time to take a drink of water and to get something to eat if you had it. I went hungry up there an awful lot—quite a bit (Raymond).

There was no time to eat, adrenaline was working overtime, and they were always moving—this was what the combat soldier at D-Day was experiencing. How could one expect to keep track of who was lost and when? Raymond further narrows down what was going through most soldiers' minds here:

> I: Either happiness or sadness? The emotions? Through the interview you've been relatively matter-of-fact, this is the way it was, but it must have been . . . ?

> R: Well you want to know? I'll tell you the truth. Me, myself,
> I didn't have time to think of anything like that. I done my
> job and I was just trying to save my skin. I was looking out
> and I was looking out for the guys. I tried to teach them
> everything I know. To keep yourself straight and sane . . .
> would I get wounded or anything. So I done the best I could.
> Cause there were young guys like me. Yeah you get some old
> guys in but they're just so reclusive. So . . . (Raymond).

And yet, many of these leaders did keep track, and with poignant words they recall events of lost comrades and reactions both at the time and afterwards. Major General (Ret.) Milnor James Roberts was the Aide de Camp to the V Corps Commander, Major General Leonard Gerow, during the landing.

> On the way across, I was chatting with another fellow who
> was my age, same rank, both captains, and both training in
> the military and civilian background. We were like two peas
> in a pod, really. I had known him before. We had a nice
> conversation. On D-Day Plus One, I had to go back to the
> beach, I don't recall what for. They had not policed up the
> bodies. I accomplished whatever mission it was, but then I ran
> across the corpse of this officer I was telling you about. I just
> happened to see him. He was lying down dead, a hole in the
> middle of his head. His crossed rifles were still on the shirt,
> his captain's bars were still on there. He's there, and I'm here,
> and I really got shaken up over that one. Five years later, I got
> in touch with, this guy's family. He had gone through ROTC
> at the University of Maryland. I was able to then identify his
> family, so I got in touch with them. I had been with their son
> (inaudible). That was an instant I'll never forget (Roberts).

Major General Roberts carried the memories of his friend for five years until he was able to discharge his duty to his friend by locating his family and perhaps giving them a small amount of peace by saying that he had been there with him, he knew him, and most importantly, remembered him. It is no small wonder that this man became a General Officer. He had the attributes of loyalty and duty, and he felt the compelling need to do this unrequested task, to somehow bring peace to the man and his family. MG Roberts also shows a level of humility, acknowledging the debt he felt, and the responsibility to keep a self-imposed contract with a friend. MG Roberts went on to become Chief of Staff of the Army Reserve from 1971 to 1975.

Ray Tolleson of Company A, 2nd Ranger Battalion was introduced in an earlier section. He was wounded on the way in to the beach. He was saved by the fast thinking of a comrade. Tolleson had been injured about 150 yards from the shore and his friend Bill Dounows patched him up while still on the beach, but Dounows then had to continue on, never knowing whether Tolleson had survived or not. Tolleson describes how forty years later, the two met up again:

> A great thing happened to me, and we had a reunion in San Diego in the 1980's and we registered for each of the Companies . . . anyway, here I am at this reunion and he was so excited because when he left me there he never dreamt that I would survive and the shock was such that I didn't know that it was even him that did it (Tolleson).

Somewhere in their minds, the information was being categorized at an incredible rate while the action was going on around them:

> Well my pathfinder team, there was only 9 of us, actually assembled, 2 of those guys were 504 men, that means only 7 were actually together on hill 30. The other guys where Nickleson was, the other half of the stick most of those guys were all killed, one of them wasn't killed until a few days later. He was shot, {and} he fell in the water and drowned before they could pull him out. That was Walter Harrelson, he was on our pathfinder team from H company. He drowned.[12] (Lamoureux).

---

[12] Although the Airborne units landed inland there were a number of drowning because the Germans had taken the pre-caution to flood the flatlands in and around various potential drop zones. The Merderet River

These kinds of details were present in nearly every lengthy account in the group studied: A quick recollection of those who were present, the circumstances, and then the actions of the individual himself. Sixty years after the fact, the memories of the men they fought with were still as vivid in their minds as they were the day the events occurred.

Others carried their responsibilities for their comrades for many years until other pieces of information became available. Once receiving such information, they acted, just as Francis Lamoureux, from the 82d Airborne did:

> One of the guys, he was probably number 12 on the stick, he was from I company, his name was Ralph Nickleson, from Nasheville, Iowa. He was only about 20 years old, young fellow, I was 24 when I jumped into Normandy. He was carrying a land mine, and as soon as his chute popped open, and when mine opened I went through about 2 or 3 oscillations and I was on the ground, that's how low we were. We were really low, and we practiced 500 feet in England, but I think this was a little less than 500 feet. But Nickleson got hit by small arms fire, mine went off and he was dead before he hit the ground. In 1987 I was in Texas, El Paso, we had a reunion, and there was a letter handed to me, his sister had written a letter to the 82nd Airborne, and from the 82nd went to about 3 or 4 or 5 hands, and asking if anyone knew, and she had heard that the 82nd was having a reunion in El Paso, Texas and she thought she could find someone who knew her brother, and who could tell her how he died, what happened to him, how he got killed. His body was brought back to the states and buried in the family plot in Nashville, Iowa, but they never knew what happened. Of course the military escort came with the body, but they couldn't tell them anything. So the letter reached me, because I was the only guy who knew him, knew he was a pathfinder. So when I got home, I called her and told her the whole story, and a lot more. She came to

was close to Ste. Mere Eglise, and many 82nd Airborne troopers, loaded down with gear perished there. (Zabecki, 2009) see me that Christmas and she stayed the weekend with me, and she still likes me because I told her all the good things about her brother. I told her he was killed instantly before he knew it. They never knew, but they were glad to know it (Lamoureux).

This happened many years after the War, yet his duty was clear to Lamoureux. Out of the multitude of events and experiences from D-day onwards, Lamoureux remembered his friend and the circumstances of his death. He found the man's sister and was able to provide closure for her. His act of compassion was another dimension of his overall composition as a leader. An observation can be made here that this came from within; it was part of his character, just as it was part of the character of many of the other leaders and survivors who made similar efforts to close chapters for the families of other comrades.

Sixty years after the fact, the memories of the men they fought with were still as vivid in their minds as they were the day the events occurred. Ralph "Doc" Widener still remembered Peter Weitkus, a medic from Texas who saved countless lives:

I: I was asking Doc here about the, some of the casualties that took place. I wanted to know, were there significant amount of medics available and triage available there on the beach area?

W: Peter Weitk, W-E-I-T-K US was {a medic who}was with the parts company. He was killed that day but he saved a lot of lives.

I: Do you know if he was ever put in for an award or anything?

W: Uhhh, I don't know. I really don't know.

I: Okay, well that's something I can check on.

W: Yea, you sure can. W-E-I-T-K US Peter.

I: Peter. Do you know maybe where he was from? United States?

W: He was from, I believe, Fort Worth, Texas.

I: So, Peter probably did a lot of triage bandaging, bullet holes.

W: I remember him attending to a lot of soldiers who had been wounded pretty seriously. And he himself was killed later in the day.

I: So he was exposed to fire.

W: Right.

I: On numerous occasions probably.

W: Right. Correct.

I: They lost a lot of medics here on D-Day.

Widener was never able to track down Weitkus' family, but he never forgot the heroism and actions of the man. As a fellow medic and leader, he carried a bit of Peter Weitkus with him and still rendered him honor, sixty years later. The action of remembering someone may not be so unusual, but with all of the other people, events and actions of the previous sixty years to have passed by and to still remember is a credit to the actions of Weitkus, as well as to Widener, who speaks so highly of him. Widener cements the presence of this trait of loyalty and duty by relating this anecdote:

> W: I'll tell you one interesting thing, when I did go ashore, the guy I was right next to, Paul Level, Paul Levelent. We were, we were going up the beach basically and I suddenly disappeared from view. I got into a ruttle. A ruttle is anything a depression in the sand from anywhere from a couple of inches up to six or eight feet. I fell inside that thing and I was completely covered. And he, he jerked me up.

67

I: Were you under water?

W: Uh-huh. Completely. I had a rifle too, even though I was a linguist.And then I, he jerked me up and then I grabbed him and thanked him and two seconds later, three seconds later, he had his head taken off his body by German machine gun fire. And he died instantly.

I: He may have saved your life.

W: He saved my life, definitely!

I: Have you ever met his family?

W: Yes I did. I went to see them. Toughest thing in the world to go and talk to a family.

I: I bet you they were pretty moved by your, by your . . . .

W: Well, I remember his mother put her arms around me and said I appreciate your coming by.

I: That must have been a tough, tough thing to do (Widener).

Ralph Widener was a leader at D-Day, and he continued to be a leader afterwards. An additional footnote to add about him here is that he actually went through basic training again at Fort Benning in the 1980's and became a regular fixture to the training companies there. At the time of the interview, he had been involved in 66 consecutive training cycles inspiring young soldiers with his dramatic accounts on leadership in battle.

Not every leader was able to rise to the occasion. Some were overcome by the events. Ray Tolleson mentions what happened to one officer from his unit:

An officer of mine that I don't like to say it, but the shock of the things got to him, and he was out of it. I tried to—I don't know how many hours I was out of it there (Tolleson).

Tolleson himself was overwhelmed by the combination of morphine, wounds and battle:

> And he gave me a shot of morphine and that also was comforting. So from that end I was able to make my way floating and so forth then with the tide and the waves and that eventually I reached the beach, and I ran into to other men from my company, a Jim Slagel (Schlagel?), who had died a few years ago. He was there and he had been hit in the back and he was paralyzed, and there was another fellow by the name of Joe Daniels. He was just full of holes floating around there and he didn't last. He died there, and there were others (Tolleson).

Tolleson continues his account, illustrating the whole experience of being wounded in the middle of the fight on the beach and making his way to an aid station:

> I: So you eventually passed out?
>
> T: Yes, that morphine and whatever happens, eventually I woke up and someone said there was a medical station up a ways and I was going to try and walk up the beach but I didn't have any strength. That sand was too much for me. And what was the weird thing, a tank was around there, and we sure didn't have tanks before, but there was one and the guy tried to drag me up onto the tank he was going up there, but by that time he had attracted too much attention from the Eighty-Eights and mortars and all that, so he told me to get out, and so I slid off. And so from there I walked up I couldn't stand in the sand on the middle of the road, feeling that nobody would waste a round on me anyway and I got up to the medical station and I was there for the rest of the day. Sometime during the evening I got out. They took me out to a ship and I was on an LST (Landing Ship Tank) and in bad shape (Tolleson).

Rebels Make Good Leaders

One of the recurring themes in many of the accounts is the emergence of the rebel streak in many leaders. A rebel streak is not attained in a classroom. In all of the accounts discussed, it surfaced when no other option was available. For example, the earlier account of Samuel Lence is not an isolated event. While not every dispute resulted in a fist fight, these leaders were willing to risk even court martial when it came to doing what they felt was necessary. In the following section we describe incidents of disobeying orders from officers, improperly obtaining and using equipment, or using personnel in ways that were not strictly by the book.

Medic Tom Scanlon got into trouble on a couple of occasions and was nearly court marshaled for ignoring orders, interfering with a mortar attack and feeding German prisoners. Scanlon is an outstanding example of so many of the heroes in the group studied. He is candid and frank, and does what he has to do to discharge his duties. Scanlon explains:

> During the time I got the Bronze Star, the enemy had a mortar set up in a house. It was set up in a door way. We put one shell in there. If you did hit them, all you could do was hit them in the arm with fallout from the walls. They had machine guns covering the one gate to get in there. They had crossfire coming in there, and that is why we had so many wounded. The guys trying to get over the hedge rows were getting hit. The lieutenant that was there comes over on the radio and says he'll direct fire into that house. He then calls in and drops that artillery right on top of us. I was screaming cease fire on the radio because we were right next to the house. They stopped and then another lieutenant come over, a mortar lieutenant, who was the guy that ran the mortars, and he said he'll call it in. He called for fire. They wouldn't fire and said to him "you goofed." He said he was on target, and that he was the mortar lieutenant and he finally got them to fire. He took me back to Major O'Malley and he said I'm going to Court Martial you. The major asked what I had done. I began telling what happened and I was loud. The lieutenant said "I'm going to do submit this soldier for Courts

Martial. Major O'Malley told him, "Stay alive as long as this man has, doing what he is doing, and you will be fine. Now get out of here, you're not going to Court Martial anybody!" Then he said to me, "Scanlon, stay away from him." I replied to the major "He nearly killed us, Sir" (Scanlon).

Scanlon showed incredible courage and strength of character in taking on the lieutenant and pushing the issue to get the mortar attacks stopped right in the middle of the fight. If he had been wrong, he would have faced severe consequences, and even if he was right, would the senior officer take his word over the lieutenant's? Scanlon continued to ride that rebellious streak when he was taking care of wounded soldiers:

It took us 24 days to get to Schoenberg. The lieutenant was going to dig in his mortars. We got in a lot of shell fire there. We had a bunch of wounded there and we had about 10 enemy soldier prisoners. I told him they were mine and I was using them and he asked why. I told him it was to carry our wounded guys out, and they did. When we got back, when we got them all out, those guys had on Overcoats. They were soaked through them. I didn't stop because I couldn't stop. I told the lieutenant to give them K rations and some water. He said "We don't feed the enemy." Regardless of his position, we did give them food and water, otherwise they wouldn't have eaten at all (Scanlon).

Photograph of medics at Normandy's beaches on June 9ᵗʰ, 1944.
(Source: http://docs.fdrlibrary.marist.edu)

Scanlon overrode what his lieutenant said and did the right thing by taking care of the prisoners. He also was practical by putting the prisoners to work to help with the wounded. His pragmatism and dedication to his mission overrode the conventions of rank or place. Tom Scanlon performed as a leader should—he did what was required to do his job and take care of his soldiers. Scanlon often had a broad way of interpreting instructions and permission while he was out doing his job as a medic:

> I had a real run in with a colonel once while trying to save soldiers who were wounded. It was in Germany. We had 10 litter bearers and we had to go and get the wounded out. He was down in a gully in a jeep and he told me to stay down there with him. He asked where my litter bearers were. I said they were down by the river water. He told me to go get them

so I can count them. I replied that I will leave them where they are. He said that I could take any vehicle I needed to get the wounded out, and his jeep driver heard him make that statement. He kept on telling me to bring them over to our position. Finally I got teed at him and called him every name in the book. The artillery observer, CPT Rosen told me you are going to get twenty years in Leavenworth. I took his jeep that had a big radio in it. I told the radio guy to get out. He refused. I reminded him what the colonel said about getting the wounded out and took the jeep anyway. When the colonel came back for his jeep, the radio man was sitting there with his radio. He asked where his jeep was and his radioman replied that the medic took it. They had one other jeep there that got stuck in the mud, and a tank went to pull him out and the mud came right over the jeep and the driver.

Later on, I saw that colonel in the Huertgen Forest when he cracked up. I asked him if he remembered me. He said "I will never forget you." But you know, he never said a word about our first encounter. All that cussing at him before, and I never heard a word about it. He could have sent me to Courts Martial, but he didn't (Scanlon).

Other situations brought out something akin to a rebellious streak, but it was more of a commentary on the leadership at the time. One disgusted junior officer, Raymond Mason, had this to say about poor leadership during the Battle of the Bulge. He did not mince his words when he spoke to his battalion commander:

Coming back down, we are all heroes, but we are not always heroes. We found an entire battalion of 155 mil howitzers abandoned in a field with its prime movers. The soldiers, the artillery men were all down the road gathered together in a field. I had our people drag some of the guns loose that were stuck. It was a sickening thing for an artilleryman to see.

When the battalion commander came out on the road and asked how the firefight was going up the road where we had just come from, I told him, with all the sarcasm that I could muster that there was no firefight. To get back there and recover his guns and they were all loose and ready to go. He left ammunition, sights, firing locks. They just abandoned everything, and bugged out. It was a "bad news" thing. As an artillery man I hate to report that but it happened (Mason).

The way that Mason makes the phrase, *"We are all heroes, but we are not always heroes,"* is a striking self-admission and revelation of the soldier and leader. Such times required leaders to be rebels occasionally, not necessarily to be heroes, but to get the mission done.

Sometimes it was not only the NCO's and Junior Officers who were rebels. Although senior leaders will be discussed in a later section, it is appropriate to recall the anecdote from the accounts of Louis Happle and Gordon Howell, (first introduced in Chapter 3, Part V.) who served together in the Navy and were present to take in wounded soldiers. The example of when the Colonel pulled up to a gangway with a wounded soldier whom he was putting in for a Medal of Honor left a permanent impression on the men of a truly caring leader. His words, at the gangway, recalled by Gordon Howell, sum up how this leader felt about his soldier and to what lengths he would go to take care of him, "And the colonel replies, "Young man, let me tell you something—I have a wounded man here that I am putting in for the Medal of Honor, and I don't want to hear anything about gangways, and I want him brought up there right now! (Happle, L. & Howell, G.)""

This exchange shows that even the highest ranking officers had to sometimes fight the system in order for the right thing to get done. In this case, the leader went to extraordinary lengths to see that the soldier he was putting in for the Medal of Honor would receive the quickest available care.

Throughout this chapter, we have examined many examples of leadership that emerged among first line leaders during the D-Day Invasion, as well as afterwards. <u>The composite picture that emerges is a leader who was diligent to his duties, loyal to his troops, compassionate, and at times rebellious when the mission called for it.</u> We have seen that leadership at the first line level is not necessarily the realm of either the enlisted soldier or the officer.

There were many examples of lieutenants showing maturity and leadership that contrasts to some thinking and stereotyping of today's lieutenants. Looking back on my own lieutenant days and up to the present, the lieutenants have been perhaps underrated and put down, often being the butt of jokes, and typically being viewed as lost and clueless. The examination of these accounts shows that the lieutenants of WWII carried themselves with honor and courage and demonstrated exceptional leadership. There is a lesson in this observation: we need to reexamine how lieutenants and junior leaders are treated and empowered. Likewise, the majority of accounts speak positively of the captains and company commanders who led these men. This was not quite so unexpected, but their fascinating accounts of leadership painted a fuller picture of what leadership on the battlefield is. The observations of how the non-commissioned officers who made up the squad leaders and platoon sergeants went to incredible lengths to get the mission done also brought a depth to what the study of emergent leadership involves. The question of why they did what they did has been partially answered in this chapter. They acted because they felt an intrinsic need to look out for those who followed them. They felt an obligation to see the mission through because they knew there was no other choice once they hit the beach or jumped from the plane. They acted out of loyalty, duty, and self-resolve for their cause, their country, but mostly for their soldiers.

This chapter focused on how first line leaders led their troops in direct roles. In the next two chapters we will look at the impact of senior leaders and how their pattern of leadership at D-Day and beyond inspired their soldiers to perform and win under harsh conditions, difficult odds, and sometimes at any cost.

CHAPTER 5

PERCEPTIONS OF OFFICERS
BY ENLISTED SOLDIERS

WE DISCUSSED OBSERVATIONS OF FIRST line leaders in the previous chapter. These leaders were primarily at the Company Grade (rank of lieutenant and captain) and below. Soldiers' perceptions of officers were generally very favorable. We noted there were some exceptions to this, but overall the group was solidly positive in their views of their officers. Additional empirical research showed that this qualitative analysis is in line with the quantitative analysis done by the Army, published in the 1949 Stouffer study.

The examples given in our study portrayed caring leaders who were on point with their soldiers. Most of the group studied was in the combat arms, and all soldiers of front line deployed units. The data from the military studies shows that soldiers who were in units that were not deployed or whose leaders did not serve alongside them, were less likely to display these same traits, and were less respected by their men.

According to *Studies in Social Psychology in World War II*, (Stouffer et al., 1949) attitudes about leaders in World War II had several phases and parallels. In the initial phase of the war, there was a generally favorable attitude about the Army. As the length of time in the Army service increased, there was a generally decreasing percentage among all ranks in positive attitudes held towards the organization. There was a similar trend among enlisted and non-commissioned officers towards officers as the war progressed. Although the authors stressed it was not a causal relationship, it does show that a level of disillusionment about the organization and its policies as a whole increased over time. The attitudinal trend among soldiers who were nearer the fighting action generally reflected more favorable attitudes towards officers than among those who were in units away from the fighting. This was most strongly reflected among combat arms soldiers surveyed (see Table 2), who showed up to a 20% higher rating for officers being willing to go through anything they had to go through, as well as for the level of personal interest in the soldiers themselves. The table below reflects this observation:

Table 2. Attitudes toward Officers among Troops in the European Theater (percentages Responding "All or Most")

	How many of the officers in your present outfit are the kind who are willing to go through anything they make their men go through?		How many of the officers in your present outfit take a personal interest in the welfare of the men?	
	Noncoms	**Privates**	**Noncoms**	**Privates**
Infantry rifle and heavy weapons companies	63%	70%	60%	61%
Other field force units	52%	58%	56%	52%
Communications Zone troops	43%	51%	51%	44%

(From *Studies in Social Psychology in World War II*, Stouffer et al., 1949, Chap. 5, p.366)

The fact that the men at D-Day were certainly in the front lines and were led by officers who had to share the same burdens, hardships, and dangers as they did validates the observations of both the survey conducted in April of 1945 and those of the accounts in our study. This also gives further validity to what the men have to say about their leaders and, since it correlates closely to the quantitative study results, lessens the likelihood that they may have embellished or softened their opinions over time.

The military study by Stouffer showed that the opinion of enlisted and NCOs who viewed officers unfavorably outnumbered that of those who viewed them favorably. But among combat units this was not the case. Indeed, in our study, most comments indicate the opposite. The data indicates that a good reason for this may be that of the men who were on the front lines, most were combat arms and were members of units with high *esprit de corps*. These factors played into their favorable attitudes about their leadership. The discipline, training and challenge of many of the units, coupled with the tone set by the leaders of such units, added to the favorable attitudes.

The Stouffer survey points out that those who were not in front line units as well as those who were not combat arms had a less favorable attitude in general about their officers. These soldiers made up the majority of the army, as there was a long trail of jobs that had to be done to provide for the infantryman, tanker, and artilleryman who made up the bulk of the front line units in the fight. Thus, despite the hardship and rigors faced by units in combat, there seems to be a bonding effect towards leaders, who had to rise to the occasion and perform more efficiently as leaders, most likely due to the austere and challenging circumstances.

A good example of this more favorable attitude towards their officers was given by Harry Brown of 2nd ID. Brown was in the engineers, not the infantry, but they were on the front lines. His unit had fewer NCOs, and he was inspired by the leadership of his lieutenant:

> B: I'd say not counting the 3rd replacement depot, with the 2nd infantry division the leadership could not be any better . . . Well, I'm a private, and I've been a private and I went into the 2nd infantry and there were four privates. And engineers by organization are not prone to be loaded too heavy with noncoms; there are usually a lot of privates and PFCs, a lot of tech T's, not too many line infantry type (Brown, pg. 14).

Signalman 2nd Class Clifford Goodall of the U.S. Navy gave his impression of one officer from the Engineer Branch. During this time he was with the 29th Infantry Division. Soon after D-Day there was a major storm that caused significant damage to the beach landing area. He describes the storm and the amount of energy the captain put into his job working to clear the harbor so ships could come in:

> That was the most awful thing I think I have seen, the piling (up) of ships was just, you can't believe the mess that thing

(storm) had left. So that particular period I was working with a captain, I believe he was with the 149th Combat Engineers his name was Capt. Hanen (Hannen?—ARK). He was a real dynamo. What we would do sometimes is blow up just to get an area open so you could bring in the ships, but during that whole period we really couldn't do much. The storm was just too bad (Goodall).

Tom "Doc" Scanlon, whose exploits were discussed in the earlier section on first line leaders, related how his commander would not support him for a pass to see his brother, who had been wounded over the skies of France. Scanlon, who had a reputation for being a rebel when necessary, was given the pass through the efforts of the chaplain. Scanlon's brother was on a B-17 and was shot down over Paris. He was rescued by a young French girl who helped him get to a hospital for surgery. Scanlon describes his brother's wound as "being a hole so big he could see his heart beat (Scanlon)." Scanlon told his commander he needed a three day pass to London. His commander was a doctor in the aid station where he worked. He turned down his request:

> So I went back in the hut and cut my stripes off and went back in there and threw them on the floor. I respectfully declared that I was going to go around you and I want you to reduce me to the rank of PVT of my own volition. I told him I am going to see my brother anyway. A military Chaplain finally got me that pass. He said I had better be back by six o'clock in the morning of the third morning. I assured him I will find out what I needed to know, and then I'll be right back. Looking back, it seems I was a rebel all the time I was in the Army. Sometimes I really had to be to save lives (Scanlon).

As a leader, Scanlon was willing to give up his position so he could go to see his brother. He showed guts and determination, as well as a combination of stubbornness and rebelliousness. His commander may have had reason to deny the pass, but perhaps a more compassionate decision would have been better. In the end, the chaplain played the key leadership role for helping Scanlon to get the pass.

These examples from different branches of service show that many officers who were on the front lines understood what was important in leading their soldier, airman, or sailor. Each example was different, but each provides a snapshot of a certain quality brought out by the realities of war. In Brown's case, his leader was competent, confident and provided a reassurance to his men, most of whom were privates and PFCs. In Goodall's case, the Engineer Captain he remembered was a real dynamo, someone who clearly had drive and the ability to get the mission done in very difficult circumstances. Finally, we see Doc Scanlon, whose commander did not see the need for a pass. However, his chaplain did see it and demonstrated effective and compassionate leadership, using his moral authority as chaplain to get the pass for him to visit his wounded brother.

This compassion and understanding was a trademark trait that showed up several times in the accounts. It must be said that the officers were not clairvoyant, but once they saw an issue, they often did the right thing for the soldier, even if it was a little bit outside regulations.

The 82nd's Daryle Whitfield's father was busy setting up a Post Office for the Navy in Casablanca during the North Africa Campaign. He took matters into his own hands to go and see his father, and instead of ending up in the stockade, a wise, caring and understanding leader let him officially go visit:

> {my}calling to duty began when my dad sailed overseas on U.S.S. George Washington. He was at Casablanca in the Navy setting up a Post Office in that area. Early on during my time overseas, I jumped the fence to try and visit my father as I didn't believe I would have been allowed to otherwise. He put me in a jeep and I returned to my company. I later on got a 3-day pass to have a good visit with dad (Whitfield).

Whitfield's commander must have made the right choice in how he dealt with him, because Daryl Whitfield went on to be wounded three times in one battle, and served in other campaigns beyond Normandy, including Market Garden and the Battle of the Bulge.

Further Perceptions of Officers in Action

Another aspect of officers in action is seen from the following extracts of data from the Stouffer study. In Table 3, 188 enlisted soldiers were asked to recall their experiences with officers who they thought did a particularly good job. The group was from soldiers who had served in the Mediterranean theater. One hundred forty-four soldiers answered the question. Comments about officers who displayed courage, encouraged men, and showed concern for them were among the most frequently mentioned of the group.

Table 3. Characteristics Displayed by Officers
Reported by Veteran Infantrymen in Mediterranean, April 1944
(reported as percentages of comments in each category)

	Percentage
Led by example; did dangerous things himself, displayed personal courage and coolness	31%
Encouraged men; gave pep talks, joked, passed on information	26%
Showed active concern for welfare and safety of men	23%
Showed informal, friendly attitude; worked along with me	5%
Miscellaneous or unclassifiable	15%

(From Stouffer et al., 1949, VOL 2, Chapter 3, p.125)

In Table 4, interviews of soldiers of all ranks were conducted in three groups numbering 260 for enlisted, 414 for noncommissioned officers, and 75 for officers. Their answers and comments relate an interesting picture of the differences between junior, inexperienced soldiers and older, more seasoned NCOs and officers. It is important to note that while younger inexperienced soldiers regarded courage and aggressiveness as premium skills, the more experienced soldiers and officers placed other attributes, such as knowledge and job performance, and leadership ability and practices at a much higher level of importance. The first set of attributes mentioned—courage and aggressiveness—correlates with the same level of importance as in Table 3, but that table does not disclose information on leadership and practices, whereas this one does. The more diverse group brought out this aspect of leadership, and suggests that more developed leaders recognize the importance of leadership ability and practices over both courage and knowledge and job performance.

Table 4 is an expanded breakdown of Table 3. It provides more information on what comprised the statements that were combined to form the generalized observations in Table 3. This is included to show the broad aspects of the variance within the general leadership attributes identified. Due to the quantitative nature of the Stouffer studies, it is helpful to include this portion to show more texture to the interpretation of the data.

Table 4. Characteristics Displayed by Officers Reported
by Rank of Veteran Infantrymen in Mediterranean, April 1944
(reported as percentages of comments in each category)

	Percentage of Comments Mentioning Each Characteristic		
	PVT/PFC	**NONCOM**	**OFFICER**
Courage and aggressiveness	59%	42%	30%
Fearless, brave, cool, "had guts," disregarded personal safety	46%	35%	21%
Displayed aggressiveness and initiative	13%	7%	9%
Knowledge/adequate performance of job	28%	19%	13%
Knew what to do and did job well	19%	9%	3%
Observant; alert; excellent on scouting and patrol work	6%	-	-
Carried out orders to the letter	3%	-	-

Used good judgment, common sense; good planner	-	10%	10%
Leadership ability and practices	8%	33%	56%
Leadership ability and miscellaneous leadership practices	2%	13%	14%
Helped other men; took personal interest in them and their problems	3%	10%	24%
Led by personal example; always with men in combat	-	9%	18%
Cheered men by humorous remarks	3%	1%	-
Miscellaneous or irrelevant	5%	6%	1%
Number of comments	N=260	N=414	N=75

(From Stouffer et al., 1949, VOL 2, Chapter 3, p.125)

Summary

The data from the Official Government Surveys from the Stouffer volumes showed that highly thought of leaders led by example, faced danger, and led the way through personal courage and acts. Additionally, the leader was someone who encouraged his men, gave pep talks, and passed on information. The third most frequent actions of leaders that enhanced their standing were when they showed active concern for the welfare and safety of the men. The study data clearly shows that the higher level of maturity and experience in both NCOs and officers correlated to a change in the perceived importance of various aspects of leadership. This study was only one of many that were conducted in the multi volume work of the Stouffer group. However, it adds an additional validation of many of the observations discussed in the current study, particularly in relation to the perceptions of the first line and senior leaders.

CHAPTER 6

THE SENIOR LEADERS

Introduction

THERE WERE MANY LEADERS WHO were both famous and infamous during the war. Countless articles, movies and books have been written about many of the well-known ones. It does not take a student of history to be familiar with names like Patton, Eisenhower, Bradley, Montgomery, and De Gaulle. Other well-known leaders from D-Daywere men like Lieutenant Colonel James E. Rudder, Commander of the 2nd Ranger Regiment, and Brigadier General Teddy Roosevelt, Jr., son of a President and Medal of Honor recipient.

In this chapter we will look at some of these men and their leadership through the lenses of the men who followed them, observed them, and saw firsthand how they handled the leadership challenge of D-Day and beyond. The first hand insights of these soldiers who observed them brings a new side to the story of these people made famous by their actions and participation at D-Day. The composite archetypes we can draw about them shows that senior leadership is not limited to a specific quadrant on a chart. Each of the officers presented in this section measures up differently in the descriptions of them. This short, cursory look at these officers provides a basis of reflection when we consider the leadership traits of the first line leaders of D-Day.

More importantly, the anecdotes from the accounts of the men who knew them and who interacted with them on a regular basis show important leadership dynamics. We will get the opportunity to look at the leadership traits that emerged among these leaders during the heat of battle, under the strain of the grueling responsibility of the campaign itself. When we look at these senior leaders, we may see some archetypical characteristics that may have been displayed in our review of the more junior, first line leaders. When we look at the profiles of them painted by the men who were there, we are not simply looking at the regurgitated words of historians. We are looking at them from the perspective of the men who marched side by side with them, who experienced their fears, pains, and triumphs.

1. The other Roosevelt—Archetype 1

FDR may have been the President, but to the men of the 4th Infantry Division, Teddy Roosevelt, Jr. held a special place in their heart. Roosevelt was one of the last of his kind: A gentleman officer who hailed from another generation that seemed to feel a certain level of *noblesse oblige* that has become somewhat absent in our society today. The book *AWOL: The unexcused absence of America's upper classes from military service* (Roth-Douquet, 2006) goes into detail about a precipitous drop in participation by the privileged of America in military life since the end of World War II. Whether it has been due to ridding campuses such as Princeton and Harvard of ROTC, or an aversion to service, men like T.R., as those familiar with history have referred to him, are fewer today than at D-Day.

One soldier from the 47th Infantry Regiment, 9th Infantry Division, PVT John Roman recalls seeing Roosevelt at the beach and spoke of him in this way:

> I: How did you feel about the leadership?

> R: Very good. The man we always looked up to was Roosevelt, with his little cane. And we had a good commanding officer . . . there were many times this man was seen up in the front leading his men. That's what I was always talking about with the soldiers, I seen him up there many a times. (Roman).

Roman speaks well of both Roosevelt and his commanding officer. Both men were up front leading the way with their soldiers. He looked up to them and felt confidence from them, and consequently managed to perform his mission and thus survive the fight. How much that re-assurance and confidence played a role in his own performance is not known, but the fact that he remembered both men and talked about them in this way suggests that there was an impact.

Carl Cannon served in the 4th Infantry Division. He was there as the invasion unfolded and the troops began landing at Utah Beach. When they arrived, this is what they experienced under the leadership of Brigadier General Roosevelt:

> I was still in the 4th Infantry Division on D-Day at Utah Beach. The landing was to the south and the stiff winds and the high waves pushed us 1000 yards too far south. We knew from the briefings how our landing looked. General Roosevelt came in and the first thing he said was "This is the wrong place."
>
> General Roosevelt talked to Colonel Johnson, Colonel Howell{and Colonel Van Fleet}, and suggested we withdraw, reload, and try and get to our designated landing point. Well, we ended up making our way in right where we landed. General Roosevelt had a walking stick in his right hand, and a 45 pistol in his left. He was directing all of us to get in to Sainte-Mère-Église and we all thought he was the best. [13]
>
> If anyone tells you they weren't afraid, they were a damn liar or a damn fool. When we hit the beach with machine gun nests, pillboxes, and artillery facing us, and soldiers all around us were getting blown in half with body parts landing in the foxholes we took up positions in, we were all terrified (Cannon).

Cannon portrays Roosevelt as a pragmatic man who understood the situation and who was willing to listen to the counsel of his advisors. He does not say Roosevelt immediately made an order to do something. His account shows a man who thought first, consulted, and then acted. Cannon describes for us a leader given a curve ball who used a measured, mature response. He did not panic, and he did not let the soldiers know if he was worried. He simply continued on with what

---

[13] COL James Van Fleet was also in attendance. The meeting was held in a small crater on Utah Beach (Zabecki, 2009).

had to be done. After discussing the options, the unit proceeded, and rather than being on board some troop ship safely away from the action, General Roosevelt was in the thick of it, walking stick in one hand, due to near crippling arthritic pain, and a .45 caliber pistol in the other. His father, former President Theodore Roosevelt, would have been proud of him if he could have been there to observe him bridge the gap between common enlisted soldiers and himself as he inspired them to perform their missions. Cannon gives a riveting picture of what they all faced with his description of the beach. The fact that he describes Roosevelt as being in the thick of things and the impression he left in this particular anecdote speak to Roosevelt's personal charisma and leadership under such conditions.

As mentioned earlier, Roosevelt was not a professional military man. He had served in World War I, but his coolness under fire and his ability in leading soldiers reflected on what the ideals of his time called for in a gentleman warrior. He was almost a mythical figure come to life, representing the American gentry. Even by World War II, such a breed was vanishing, being supplanted by the incredible rate of accessions of ROTC and OCS graduates. According to Stouffer, World War II saw a change in the attitudes about officership in general, especially in terms of the stratification and separation between officers and enlisted. This two-volume study was published in 1949 and taken from studies done throughout and immediately after the war. It marks the changes that were realized by the time that I entered the military in 1992, and which were certainly evident in 2008. Thus, Roosevelt was a man and a leader who worked with consideration for others and used empowering techniques before the buzzwords of situational leadership and other terms appeared in the lexicon of leadership. Another example of this is given by 4th Infantry Division medic Tom Scanlon, whom we have already discussed and profiled. In it, he references Roosevelt singing a ditty from the First World War, where he served in the 1st Infantry Division:

> I saw Roosevelt in Val, he was with a soldier from H Company who was a WWI Veteran, and they were both drunk as skunks. They were arm in arm singing *"Mademoiselle from Armentières"* Right after that he died of that heart attack. I know where they said he was killed but they told us he died of a heart attack. He was a good ole boy, walking with that

stick cane and singing that *"Mademoiselle from Armentières"*. The soldiers would wave to him and talk with him. They liked him. He was a hell of a soldier (Scanlon).

Another of Roosevelt's men of the 4th Infantry Division, Armand Torre, described the landing with Roosevelt:

> We stayed out on the water for a long time before we finally hit the beach. We really didn't know what we were getting into. When the word came, we just went over the side and got into the water. My regiment, the 12th Infantry Regiment of the 4th Infantry Division went in third on the 6th of June 1944.

> Fellows were getting hit. General Roosevelt was our Division Commander[14] and he was down there on the beach directing things and I admired him. We all did. When he died, it didn't really affect what we had to do but we felt our loss of him (Torre).

He was a "hell of a soldier" and leader. He had the ability to transcend rank and class and be one of the men; but at the same time he also had the other requisite traits needed by men who made the tough decisions. The everlasting testimony to this remarkable man was that he was awarded the Medal of Honor for his gallantry during the D-Day landings.

Roosevelt's inclusion here is not simply because he was mentioned, nor because he was the son of a famous President. It was because he was a senior leader whose leadership traits emerged on the battlefield at the critical time and place and added to the momentum necessary to carry the day at Normandy.

---

[14] Brigadier General Theodore Roosevelt, Jr. was in fact the Assistant Division Commander. The 4th Infantry Division Commander was Major General Raymond Barton.

<u>Roosevelt—Perceived Leadership Composite—Archetype 1</u>

- ➢ Thoughtful
- ➢ Measured
- ➢ Collaborative
- ➢ Accessible
- ➢ Respected
- ➢ Courageous
- ➢ Human

2. Patton—The Rebel General—Archetype 2

There are many stereotypes and images of the American military leader; but few are more familiar than General George S. Patton. Patton's leadership style left an indelible mark on the military. He is important to this study not only because his soldiers admired him, but also because he represents a prime example of one of the observations of emergent leadership—the rebel. While there are a lot of people today who use the phrase, "outside the box thinking," the fact is that Patton and those like him did not simply think outside of the box, they changed the box into a new form. Many leaders thought outside the box and were successful; many thought and acted within the box and were successful, as well. Patton was like our first line leaders who pushed their parameters to the limit, sometimes crossing the line, but doing so in a way that made sense and ultimately was forgivable. Patton's well known history is not perfect, and his men do not recall him through a rose-colored glass. However, ultimately they admired him for his flash, dash and desire to accomplish the mission, as well as his willingness to do what had to be done. The theme of "we did what we had to do, we just kept going, someone had to do it, you just kept going," all phrases found throughout the accounts, shows a dogged determination to get things done.

Patton was at the extreme end of that scale. His leadership earned him great respect on the battlefield; his victories occurred through personal presence and force of will. Just as Teddy Roosevelt, Jr.'s, presence cheered and encouraged the men at Utah, so too, did General Patton's presence have an effect as a force multiplier for his men. Germans were absent their key general, Field Marshal Rommel, and so they were missing their own leader around whom to rally. The breakout in Normandy occurred once the Allies finally let Patton loose. His troops, along with other American and Allied forces, successfully battered their way through Northern France. As a leader, he was willing to take the chances he felt were necessary to get the job done. This resulted in overextending his lines and running out of fuel, but he somehow managed to get enough done to drive the German War machine further back and out of France. Based on the accounts of the men who were there, Patton still came out of it all larger than life.

The tiny town of Dysina in the Czech Republic celebrates his final victory campaign each year. They commemorate the end of World War II with a day of speeches and remarks at the school named in his honor, under a statue of Patton that is as controversial as the man was himself. I personally attended the dedication of the statue. It was originally commissioned by the Lord Mayor of the much larger and famous city of Pilzen, home of the original Pilsner brand of beer. In the excitement of the post-cold war Czech Republic, it seems the mayor forgot that the artist commissioned to do the statue was alleged to have been a former Communist informer. Whether true or not, it created enough of an issue that the mayor of the small town of Dysina, Madame Kuklikova, was able to get the statue moved to her little village, which was the furthest east that Patton and his Third Army were allowed to go. Dysina boasts a second monument, one to Major General Ernest Harmon, who was also an area commander there. But it was General Patton who everyone came to see for the 60th Anniversary of the end of World War II in May 2005. Third Army sent a color guard of soldiers. At least two busloads of octogenarian veterans and their wives came to pay their respects. The May weather had taken a turn for the worse, and a stiff breeze and light rain fell as the speeches from Czech dignitaries went on and on. The small color guard stood firm and proud as the colors blew in the wind. The representative from Third Army was COL William Kane, who was missing his daughter's college graduation to represent the unit that Patton led. The most stirring thing of all was seeing the veterans all standing at attention at that moment. The sun managed to finally peek through the clouds just at the conclusion of the words of George Patton Waters and the unveiling of the statue. It shone down for a few minutes on a gleaming bronze statue, larger than the larger than life Patton himself, and then was covered over by the clouds again. Patton gazes longingly to the east to Prague, the city he was not allowed to take. The Russians got that opportunity, and more than 60 years later the inhabitants are still bitter, at least the many Czechs that I have met in my four trips to the region since then.

If it seems a bit contradictory in this discussion of Patton, it is because one cannot discuss him in simple language. I have had the good fortune to meet some of the men who were there with him and hear them tell their stories first hand. I was privileged to meet his grandson as well. Not surprisingly, the Veterans at D-Day mentioned him quite often, though he did not show until several weeks after the start of the invasion. He was part of the diversion that made the attack on Normandy so successful and added to the confusion of the Nazi High Command, as they expected him to lead the invasion.

The accounts show that Patton was as real as the stories portrayed him. The rebel first line leaders had a kindred spirit in Patton—he was one of them, except he was a general! It did not matter whether one was an infantryman or a pilot. Patton was present in the recollections of many of the veterans interviewed for this research.

Take, for example, Naval 2nd Lieutenant Frederick Crispin's and Corporal Harry L. Browne's experiences. Their Normandy Campaign experiences involved ferrying troops to D-Day and afterwards providing supplies for Patton and his Army on the move:

> Crispin: No, we left England. We started using the airstrip over here at Sainte-Mère-Église. We were making missions to that temporary airfield for about two weeks, and then we were moved out of England about July to Allenthal. Then we conducted missions resupplying Patton's 3rd Army with gears, socks, and K-rations (Crispin).

Browne added more details:

> Troop carriers did more than carry paratroopers, and pull gliders. We hauled 55 gallon cans of gasoline and all kinds of supplies. We chased Patton's Army with a lot of gasoline. We would land in cow pastures and Patton moved too fast for us to catch him at times, and our C-47 would have to get back in the air with all the gas still on board. Landing and taking off between those hedgerows was always a tough one.

Patton would stop from time to time because he kept running out of gas and bullets. We would eventually catch up to him and he would give us wounded as we offloaded the things he needed. We lost two planes because they failed to clear a hedgerow and they went down with all their men and cargo (Browne, H.).

The 439th's Phil Hecker and Alfred Lilja both described the demanding Patton as someone who also recognized his men for their hard work and efforts. In one instance, they had been transporting hundreds of cans of gasoline to grass landing strips. This is Hecker's vivid recollection:

One day we returned to the base, and the crew chief opened the back door as I swung the airplane to park it. A 6X6 backed up and unloaded a case of Piper Heit champagne for each member of the crew and there were four of us. All that the driver said was "courtesy of General Patton." The man had flash and dash. He may have had a bad reputation, but I think he was great. He did what had to be done (Hecker).

One would add to Hecker's words that Patton not only was admired for his flash and dash; but also, and more importantly, he was admired for his skill and competence.

Alfred Lilja was also the recipient of Patton's gratitude:

As the invasion grew into full swing during July, we would haul supplies and even gasoline for General Patton. General Patton was grateful in that he left us champagne and cognac (Lilja).

Patton was anxious to move because he was trying to beat the German Army and cut it off before it could retreat to the next line of defense along the Rhine frontier. According to MG (Retired) Raymond Mason, the 4th Armored Division played a major role in the breakout at Perrier. The unit was re-directed to attack at Vanes, where a submarine base was located. The action was protested by the commanding officer, General Wood, but Mason says that the famous slapping incident in Italy was still recent, and the general was unable to get the order changed:

We were ordered to attack toward Vanes and the submarine pens. No job at all for an armored division. General Wood protested to General Patton, and Patton agreed with him. But I read in history that Patton was worried about General Bradley because of that slapping incident in Italy. He didn't want to argue with Bradley too much. Bradley would not let him change because the plan called for the armor division to attack toward the "pig pens." The U boats were behind all sorts of concrete and embankments and rapidly could shoot us up. That didn't make sense. We stopped and finally got turned around and chased the Germans across France.

The 4th Armored Division led the Third Army in the middle and on the flanks. Patton was asked if he was worried about his flanks, but he was not worried about his flanks. He could take care of that and the fighter bombers helped him out (Mason).

Some of his men were aware of some of what was going on. Others were surprised to later find out that they were also diversions in the plan, just as Patton himself had been a diversion prior to the invasion. One example of this was recounted by T4 Sergeant Norman Schein of the 248th Engineer Battalion. He was one of thirty-six recon teams that Patton had sent out to gather information for a move to the South. The only problem was, there was not going to be a move to the South, it was a deliberate ploy to mislead the enemy. Schein, however, overcame the odds and actually made it back to his own lines:

Patton came up with an idea. He called in thirty-six recon teams of the Army. My partner and I were selected to go. A major general told us: "You men are going to do a vital bit of recon for us. You are going to recon the southern part of France {along} the Brest peninsula. We want to go down there and knock out that submarine base . . ." and they divided us into thirty-six sectors and my partner and I got a sector. When we left our company, we were told to bring water, gas, and food for at least ten days to two weeks . . . (Schein)

Only fourteen of the recon teams made it back. The teams that were caught had information that the Germans used to make the decision to move their troops to the South. Instead, Patton took his forces and proceeded to move in another direction, along with other Allied units as they proceeded to close a pincer movement that surrounded the German Seventh Army at Falaise-Argenten (Zabecki). However, Schein was unaware of the plan, and may never have understood the role he played in it. He was upset at how his life and that of his comrades had been endangered:

> . . . Well we found out we were expendable . . . I was pretty mad for quite awhile. I understood his strategy, but we were smart enough to get out of it (Schein).

The results of Patton's and the rest of the Allies' efforts were to successfully liberate Normandy and Paris. 1st Lieutenant Robert Landis, of the 47th Infantry Regiment, recalls the event:

> I very well remember the march . . . the 79th Division marched 130 miles by foot and rode 50 miles by truck in 72 hours. It was never done before and hasn't been done since . . . they did it to put us in an area down there because we were supposed to be help liberate Paris . . . many of us believed then and still believe, that it was political, then De Gaulle went in and liberated Paris along with Patton and some of his tanks (Landis).

Historians such as Ambrose debate whether Patton was right and should have been allowed to go forward with plans he had to cut off the German forces and punch through into Germany before they could re-group. But General Eisenhower would not allow it to happen. Army GI Robert Tate of the 9th Infantry Division said that they went to St. Lo and from there they made a hole in the enemy line so that Patton's tanks could get through and race across France. They did so until they ran short of fuel[15]:

---

[15] Author's note: Although lack of fuel was one of the ways that he was held back, and why the men in the accounts kept referring back to it, there were

> General Patton got his tanks through and raced across France.
> At times we would catch up with him but eventually he had
> to quit because he was short on gas (Tate).

Patton's leadership showed up on the battlefield in ways that were different than leadership actions of other leaders are described. There was a sense of urgency and competitiveness, combined with the rebelliousness that was part of his persona. The soldiers recognized this, and were part of his machine that carried out operations—for better or for worse. He displayed gratitude towards those who helped to sustain his efforts, but he was not afraid to put men out as bait, for the good of the cause. Such actions today might endure more scrutiny from the press and might have more ramifications, but during World War II, there was a lot at stake and decisions made then might not be made today.

<u>Perceived Leadership Composite of General Patton—Archetype 2</u>

➢ Competitive
➢ Outside the box thinker
➢ Rebel
➢ Risk Taker->Reckless
➢ Grateful/Appreciative
➢ Larger than life
➢ Stubborn

3. General Bradley—Leadership on the beach under fire—Archetype 3

General Omar Bradley was an important presence at D-Day and throughout the entire European Campaign. Many of the men who related their personal recollections of the event also recall Bradley and his impact on them. General Bradley was a more measured leader than General Patton, and at the same time he was accessible to the troops, just as BG

---

many other factors that went into Eisenhower's planning for the overall strategic victory, that the men at this level were unaware.

Roosevelt had been. He was senior in rank to both of them and was closer to the flagpole, (Eisenhower), since he was the senior American General in the invasion force. Roosevelt came from an American family institution. He was a gentleman warrior. Patton was a professional military man who came from a line of military men. Roosevelt represented the old family wealth of New York; Patton hailed from a Southern Gentry Tradition and attended Virginia Military Institute. Enter Omar Bradley, a common man who was known as the G.I.'s General. Bradley was charged with incredible responsibilities, but he was nonetheless still almost a "regular Joe" to the soldiers who knew him.

General Bradley was at Omaha Beach at 1030 hours on June 7th, 1944 when a German plane, a captured Spitfire, strafed the beach. [16] If Bradley had been hit and killed, who knows what would have happened in the following weeks. Fortunately he was not hit and he went on to his place in history. Private John Paulson of the 9th Infantry recalls the event in this interview. Paulson had always remembered Bradley and the event, but he was never sure. It was not until 60 years later that his thoughts on that day were confirmed:

> I saw a Spitfire coming right at us . . . He let go and he strafed the beach and as he went by me—by that time I was laying on the ground. I looked up and was probably not more than a hundred yards from the plane and it had swastikas all over it. So apparently, it was a captured English Spitfire. When I got up at the top of the hill there, I looked over and I thought I recognized Omar Bradley. I'd never met the man, naturally, you know being just a Private First-Class. He was over by a command car. There were half a dozen people there but I recognized him. I don't know why but it just struck me because I always thought he was such a good officer . . .

---

[16]   As incredulous as it sounds, German Forces had captured British Spitfire Airplanes (Mk.I AZ-H) during the course of the War. We cannot be entirely sure that Paulson's account refers to one of these, but there is evidence of some of these planes being captured by the Germans near Cherbourg, prior to the Invasion. Specific examples are shown at http://www.luftwaffe-experten.org/forums/index.php?showtopic=310. See also APPENDIX C: ii Photos.

So that was sixty years ago, approximately, and I never really knew for sure if it was Bradley. Then I got this magazine and it showed a picture of Bradley at Omaha Beach at ten-thirty in the morning on June 7th. So I carried this memory sixty years and I often wondered if I was right or wrong until I saw the photo in Time Magazine and that proved I was correct (Paulson).

As a young private, Paulson observed Bradley on the beach as a respected high-ranking leader and said in his words, that he "always thought he was such a good officer." And it was the elder veteran, John Paulson, who sixty years later still looked at him with great admiration. He kept that memory with him for so many years. And, of the memories and recollections of Paulson, Bradley stood out as the senior leader who impacted him the most.

What made Bradley so well liked and respected by his soldiers seems to have been the way he personally dealt with them. One example of this is from William McNamara, the war correspondent:

A big high point for us was when General Bradley gave personal thanks to my team for raising the morale of the American forces and keeping everyone informed. This was the job we were there to do, and when we got his thanks—that told us that we made a difference (McNamara).

Bradley was a leader with incredible responsibilities. Though initially the Invasion on D-Day was a success, the campaign had stalled after weeks of stubborn fighting with Germans. The St. Lo breakout was critical to the success of the campaign. General Bradley had the responsibility to execute the plan that he had developed for the breakout. It got off to a shaky start. In a later section we will look at how soldiers perceived and demonstrated leadership in two key events. Irving Smolens of the 29th Field Artillery Battalion, 4th Infantry Division experienced events at Slapton Sands and St. Lo. He recalls setting up his 155 mm guns (Smolens called these Long Toms) to support the infantry as it attacked St. Lo:

I set up my gun position to support the infantry attack. The P-47's were dropping smoke bombs to mark the target.

They called the road that was getting the smoke bombs the "St. Lo Terrier Highway" which was very narrow, and when the smoke cleared we were supposed to be on one side of the highway and the Germans were supposed to be on the other.

When the smoke began drifting back towards our own lines, the Air Force didn't read the roads correctly as another road had appeared. We all were hit pretty bad by our own bombers that day. A three-star general, General Lesley MacNiele {Author's note: LTG Lesley J. McNair}was killed there. The battalion commander called General Bradley's headquarters and said we had been decimated by the bombing and couldn't break out (Smolens).

Despite the call from the battalion commander, Bradley ordered them to attack and the unit went forward into what has become known as the "St. Lo breakthrough".

Bradley had to make the tough call to try an un-doctrinal attack tactic using infantry divisions in front instead of going with armored divisions first. According to Smolens, he did this because of the hilly terrain that was around them. This was compounded by the pressure of having had hundreds of his soldiers, including senior officers, killed in the pre-attack bombing. He had to be flexible in his thinking, and at the same time he had to be resolute and continue with the attack, despite the self-inflicted losses caused by the confusion from the smoke drifting into the allied lines.

Robert Landis recalled the experience of being one of those men who Bradley ordered forward at St. Lo:

I remember when one of our own airplanes bombed us and killed six hundred of our men. I know it was unintentionally, but we were trying to break out of the hedgerows and they pulled us back about a mile. At that time the 1800 bombers came over and started dropping bombs on the German lines. The wind blew the smoke back on us and the bombers behind them started dropping bombs on us and killed General McNair and I believe a colonel from the Air Force who was in communications with the bombers. So they lost communications with them, and the following bombers had no idea of who they were bombing. They were just dropping bombs on the smoke and dust. Finally, somehow in about an hour they got it stopped. The men of course were wounded—a lot of them. The bombs had disoriented a lot of them so I just grabbed what men I could get a hold of and we had to advance. We got to our old position and I got about a hundred yards past that and I got hit with an airburst so . . . . that's when I left the Company (Landis).

The Landis and Smolens accounts show the direct on the ground results of what men like Bradley planned and ordered. From the accounts, one can imagine that Bradley was hit with tremendous pressure, possible guilt, and the need to keep going despite what had happened. The situation was more a reflection of the early tactical integration problems than bad planning on Bradley's part. Nevertheless, as the leader he took the only steps he could—he ordered the attack to continue. This was, on a grander scale, similar to the same experiences of the soldiers themselves—they just kept going. They did what they had to do. In Bradley's case he was ordering thousands of men into battle, knowing full well that many had already been killed; but he also was aware that all of the effort and preparation that had gotten them all to that point might have been wasted if the Germans were able to contain them any longer. A failed invasion would have resulted in delaying victory in the West, perhaps allowing the Germans to fare better against the Soviets, and resulting in even more deaths. Bradley's breakout, while not an absolute necessity for the success of this invasion, was a crucial part of it. It is interesting that Bradley, who was not known for flash and dash like Patton, was referred to almost as a governor on Patton's motor during his mad dash through France. But, at the critical time and place Bradley acted, and he did so without hesitation acting decisively and deliberately.

General Bradley ultimately appears to be in his own mold. He was a man with a more humble beginning than many of his contemporaries. He often had to make difficult choices on the battlefield; but he still maintained a level of connectedness to his men and his roots.

<u>Perceived Leadership Composite of General Bradley—Archetype 3</u>

- ➢ Conservative
- ➢ Personable
- ➢ Responsible
- ➢ Grateful/Appreciative
- ➢ Firm
- ➢ Decisive
- ➢ Resolute

Summary of the Senior Leaders

The accounts of the D-Day 60 veterans included references to senior leaders, many of whom were famous outside of the event. The composites of the accounts we have reviewed show that these three leaders possess many of the same traits displayed by the first line leaders. We see such varied traits as personal accessibility, decisiveness, resolve, courage, risk-taking and outside the box thinking. Doc Scanlon and General Patton would have been able to exchange more than a few stories.

We also saw that there were differences among them and that successful senior leaders were not all cut from the same cloth—that is, they approached their men and missions differently. Their men looked at them differently. Some people might say that, of course, there are going to be differences among the leaders; but that may be news to some educational, military, and corporate thinkers who put such stock in personality testing, standardized review forms and other placement tools that size people up based on the results. Our look at the senior leaders has shown that they had many visible differences. Thus, one conclusion that can be drawn from this is that there are many variances in personality, background, and experience that can come together to shape successful senior leaders. Another is that when the big decisions had to be made, these men made them and faced the consequences with the same confidence, whether it was on the beach waving a cane, at St. Lo in the breakout, or on the country roads of France running out of gas.

4. Other Leaders: Majors and Above

After looking at the first line leaders, and then at the senior leaders, we will now look at the field grade officers (majors, lieutenant colonels), and higher, and see what leadership patterns were observed among them.

The examples of officers who were not as well publicized as men like Patton, Bradley or Roosevelt are just as important from the standpoint of the junior soldiers. The colonel, or the old man as he is often called, sets a tone and influence within a unit that goes all the way to the company level. Such applications are true today whether it is a male or female commander. One should keep this in mind when discussing leadership from the World War II, which was pre-dominantly male, but not exclusively so. In this study, however the leadership was nearly exclusively male.

In this section we will look at the examples of these leaders and see if they also displayed or were perceived to have displayed similar traits. Among the leadership traits we have discussed already, we have seen leaders who were diligent to their duties, loyal to their troops, compassionate, at times rebellious when the situation called for it, and that also includes men who held different perspectives, thought in different ways, and seized the opportunity to make a change when the situation called for it. The same traits are evident in other leaders.

Take for example, Major General Elwood "Pete" Quesada, whose innovativeness helped synchronize the Land and Air fight for the American troops. Airman Arnold Franco was in the 3rd Radio Squadron Mobile, Ninth Air Force, during World War II. He was a code breaker attached to a secret unit that was listening to enemy coded broadcasts during the invasion. He presented his views on the impact of such leadership in his interview with MAJ Douglas Hendy in 2004:

> I: Is there anything else that you would like to add before we end quotes? Something for the soldiers if this is published? The purpose of the publication would be to allow current soldiers to prepare themselves for the next war, as well as our current war.

F: Yes, I have to say, Sir . . . [17] One of the crutches (?) of the military has always been they are always fighting the new war with the tactics of the old. But there are exceptions. We were part of a superb air-ground team. A general by the name of Quesada, I don't know if you have heard of him, Pete Quesada. He had developed this, kind of that which we are using now; he put Air Force fighter pilots in tanks. And, he developed communications, radio communications, so they could communicate directly with the squadron leaders above. So an Air Force guy in the tank was talking to his own guys up there, which was . . . it sounds simple . . . it was unique. It was unique. And that created this fantastic ability that the forward Army had. The dash thru France, but forget about strikes. Because there were guys driving in tanks, who are passengers, Air Force men, who had squadrons of fighters, fighter-bombers on-call all the time. It took them years to recapitulate that fantastic type of communications (Franco).

Quesada was an outside the box thinker who applied his ideas to the battlefield with great results. As a senior leader, he broke new ground that substantially aided the Allied success. Another innovation was seen in the Hedgerow fight. While General Quesada made his impact in the communications between tank and plane, other GIs were making their impact on the ground unit by unit with their ideas.

This same dynamic was seen in first line leaders as well. Take for example the recollection by the 101st Airborne's Cletus Sellner. Sellner worked in the rigging department, the place where they were responsible for packing parachutes. The work was done in a big packing shed. The work was tedious, with each chute being packed to fit the shoulder harness for each jumper. Sellner recalls that there were injuries because the equipment weighed so much:

---

[17] Arnold C. Franco spent ten years researching use of codes during World War II and wrote Code to Victory, by Arnold C. Franco, as told to Paula Aselin Spellman Manhattan, Kan.: Sunflower University Press, c1998.

There were a lot of soldiers who ended up with broken legs, broken ankles, broken shoulders—everything because the equipment weighed 65 pounds, plus the parachute with the musette bag on top made it a bit more. A lot of people broke legs and all kinds of different injuries.

So as a result of these mishaps . . . our sergeant that was in charge of the rigger department . . . his name was Sergeant Lancey . . . designed this unit so that when the parachute opened the cord would drop using the snap release and the bag would dangle ten feet below the feet of the paratroopers. So that saved all kinds of broken legs and you name it. That was a lifesaving device that we developed over there (Sellner).

It is no accident that leadership dynamics at the senior level have parallels at the first line leader level. Perhaps it has to do with the span of control within one's own direct situation, but the end result is that innovative thinking was not something that was taught in the classroom. Both situations required action to be taken in order to successfully solve a problem. It did not matter whether it was in the fighter plane or on the way down in the parachute or in the tank beside the driver. The necessity for action was the catalyst for the ideas to come forward.

One important aspect of the senior leader is the tone that he set. In the thick of the fight, Royal British Navy LT. Michael D'Alton recalled, "And we stayed there for a few hours, waiting further orders. And suddenly my English captain declared to hell with this bloody nonsense, I'm going in. And, he ordered up anchor" (D'Alton). This officer was a man of action. He was not content to sit and watch the action without doing his part, regardless of the consequences. D'Alton picked up on that and jumped into the work down below as they were working on un-jamming the door of the landing craft when it was making its way toward the beach.

Harry Browne, of the 439th Troop Carrier Group (TCG) was a pilot on a C47 who flew missions over Normandy throughout the Campaign. He had this to say about his senior leader and the tone he set:

I was always satisfied with my chain of command. Our commanding general was a good guy, too. His leadership helped us to keep our minds on what we needed to do and even though we would lose planes and their crews from time to time—we still kept our resolve for the job we had to do. We never had anybody that made life miserable for us . . .

Yet, we were still all very close during those times. If we knew we did a good days work for the war effort, which was most of the time, we all got together back at the barracks and found time for a beer and celebrate our successes, and praise those who did not return home (Browne).

Browne's memories of the war were shaped by the attitude of his chain of command. The focused leadership of his general made him confident in his mission, and he did not worry about less important things and distractions that might have weakened his resolve or taken his mind off of what had to be done. This positive leadership example stayed with him throughout the war and lent a strong *esprit de corps* to the unit and a bond that kept the men together in friendship long afterwards.

Robert Martin Piper had memories of the exceptional leadership he experienced while in the 505th Parachute Infantry Regiment, 82nd Airborne Division. This unit has a storied history. But, this was because of the tone of leadership set by men like Major General Matthew B. Ridgway and Brigadier General James M. Gavin. The effect of outstanding leadership created an environment where others who had the desire, discipline, and traits to endure the rigorous training and standards of the Airborne unit were able to form a strong and cohesive bond that served to motivate and pull them through the challenges they faced—both individually and collectively. Piper recalls one critical test for this leadership when he and the 505th went into action on D-Day. The unit's drop zone was Sainte-Mère-Église. Once there, Piper was given the task of organizing the defense of the CP (command post) by his commander, Colonel William Eckman in one of the typical Normandy apple orchards. He recalls Colonel Eckman as being one of the best things to happen to his unit, the 505th PIR (Parachute Infantry Regiment). Piper landed in a farm west of Sainte-Mère-Église. He recalled the peaceful night, the dog barking in the background, and the moonlight. In his words, "Other than the war, it was a very peaceful night (Piper, p. 188)." Piper's opinion of his chain of command was high. The small Division CP was bordered by hedgerows. The Division was using the Regimental CP since it was the only established CP at the time on the ground. Manned by 25 soldiers, Piper said they were constantly tired, but that the defense was, "like a hornets nest" against enemy probes, "Everyone in our outfit knew what they were doing, and the troops performed their jobs outstandingly (Piper)." It was the tone and standards set by men like Ridgway, Gavin, and their immediate subordinate leaders, like COL Eckman and LTC Kraus and others that made the unit what it was.

Although the first line leaders who made up the bulk of the veterans in the survey were important in carrying out and executing missions on the ground, it was the higher rung of officers who set the tone, set the stage for training, as well as providing the guidance and fine tuning through personal presence to lead the troops successfully in the fight.

CHAPTER 7

SPONTANEOUS EMERGENCE OF GROUP LEADERSHIP

Introduction

IN THE PRECEDING SECTIONS WE discussed the presence of leadership traits in first line leaders, famous senior leaders, and unit senior leaders identified in the accounts of our group of veterans. These leadership examples were under the formal organizational structure at various levels. The impact of the first line leader was shaped by many factors. One factor was the leadership examples set by those in command at the highest level. Another was that of the tone set in an organization, such as in the 101st Airborne Division and the 82nd Airborne Division. The examples, tone and expectations affected how the organizations as whole conducted business.

The next section discusses leadership traits that emerged as a result of circumstances at the small group level rather than the unit level. What leadership occurred when it was small groups of men, sometimes from various units, as they came together to overcome challenges before them? The distinction between this and first line leadership is that in first line leaders, we looked at junior level and company grade formal authority structures. In this section, we will look at *ad hoc* structures and clusters that emerged out of the chaos of D-Day and other events, and how an almost natural sequence of leadership assumption occurred as a result of the combination of events, circumstances, training and traits of the leaders involved. In some instances, people acted because of training; in others they acted in their formal roles. But, what happened most often was that one member of the group on impulse decided to act, take charge, or direct his fellow soldiers when an event presented itself. Many times, this occurred in the most unlikely circumstances, and the veteran presenting the account describes himself as surprised that he did it or asked himself "what was I thinking?" afterwards.

Spontaneous Leadership

What is spontaneous leadership? One definition could be the emergence of leadership actions in the moment of crisis when action must be taken, often being the difference between death and survival for those who suddenly come together to form a group, no matter the length of time. Another might be the sudden emergence of someone who is the instigator or troublemaker in a group, and may at times be in benign, although reckless situations.

The 82nd Airborne's Will Delaney describes this process in his account of the D-Day jump he and his fellow soldiers made. They flew in at 700 feet, leaving early on the the 5th of June, but their flight was delayed 24 hours. Delaney describes a chaotic scene on the ground. Men were caught in trees, and a couple in church steeples:

> We were the lead aircraft, the "pathfinder" and we finally jumped at 1:30 in the morning of the 6th. I was in 2nd Battalion, F Company 505th Parachute Infantry Regiment. John Steel and SGT Brown ended up landing on top of a church steeple. SGT Brown got away but John Steel stayed up there (Delaney).

Once on the ground, Delaney linked up with his friend Francis Meeks from Alabama and the two soon realized they were in the wrong town. They used their "cricket" (the device designed for the invasion force to establish contact with each other via clicks and counter clicks) and met another soldier, a SGT Hill, who hailed from California. Hill had been caught in a tree by his harness. Hill had been shot; but the bullets had not gone through his reserve shoot, thus saving his life. Soon afterwards they met up with Lieutenant Carol and the party was soon under fire from the tree line nearby. As Delaney says "we realized we were definitely not in a good place (Delaney)."

After another 100 yards, they were met by Lieutenant Colonel Kraus, who told them they were in the wrong place. The lieutenant told Kraus that they were heading for high ground. The group slowly grew to over 20 personnel making their way undercover, walking most of the night. Delaney recalls what happened next:

> As daylight broke, we came to "Monaberg Station" and we
> knew that there was no way we were supposed to be there.
> We turned around and made our way back in the other
> direction, and picked up 20 more men along the way . . .
> when we finally arrived back into Sainte-Mère-Église during
> the afternoon of June 6th, our company had formed up right
> next to the graveyard in the spot I had landed on in the dark
> (Delaney).

Delaney does not give specific details on where the men who joined
the group came from. He notes that the battalion commander was
focused on his mission and they were focused on theirs. When they got
to town, they broke into small groups and did house to house fighting.
Thus at one point or another throughout the process, nearly every soldier
was both a leader and a follower.

Thomas Alley, who came from the 101st Airborne Division describes
his encounter with German soldiers and members of an informal group
that came together after landing in Normandy. Alley and two other men
with him heard the squeaking wheels of a cart being pulled by a donkey
being led by five German soldiers. One sergeant took an automatic
weapon from the lead German soldier. A second German fought back,
hit the sergeant with a leather donkey whip and from a few feet away
Alley shot him with his M-1 carbine. The sergeant from the 82nd fired
on the other soldiers and killed them. Alley and his comrades quickly
moved on and met another group of seven men. The men had heard the
shooting and wondered what had happened since they could tell it was
a German weapon by the rate of fire. The small group moved on. Alley
sums up the anecdote this way:

> The guy from the 82nd who was timely with that automatic
> weapon went another direction with more 82nd guys that
> appeared from a field and I never saw him again (Alley).

The group came together out of necessity, formed for a few hours,
forever bonded by an incident and then dispersed with little more
information directly passed perhaps than the exchange of names.
Another account of the spontaneous team forming and coming together

for a short time and then breaking off and forming up with other groups is given by Alley's fellow member of the 101st, Eugene Cook. After his parachute landing Cook met up with a soldier from the 502nd PIR, later on they met seven or eight others and headed down the road nearby to Ravenoville.

> We had two point-men, but when we got up to them they were both gone. One had been captured, and we don't know what the hell happened to the other . . . We got to the town and surveyed it a bit. I think there were twenty-two of us actually in the town. That was early in the morning. It took about two hours to capture it. I don't know, but I think there were about two hundred Germans in that town . . . It was more house-to-house fighting; it was a small town. You would throw a grenade in this window, then walk in. We had twenty-two guys who went house to house and the town. We were fighting individually, or in groups of two or three. That took about two hours and then we took some prisoners and took them back to the church. This was at about seven o'clock in the morning . . . that lasted all of D-Day, into the night. The next morning we headed for our drop zone, where we were supposed to be. So that was D-Day (Cook).

Cook's group of men came together, and they were able to form a squad and move as a unit and then went on to attack a town. Following that, they went on to link up with the rest of the units. As noted by Cook, he did not know what happened to the original point men that joined the group, yet for a short period of time they were an integral part of the group.

Rollo Worden talks about the difficulties of holding his squad together, and gives this anecdote about events he experienced during the Battle of the Bulge:

> After Bastogne, we were trapped in an old mill for several days until we snuck out one night. There were 18 of us left out of three Companies. There would be forty of us at times from ten different outfits. We didn't know where we were most of the time or what we were doing, but eventually we finally ended

up in Bavaria . . . We rode tanks with Patton's tanks for four or five weeks. When they got fired on, we jumped off those tanks and lost a lot of men along this trail with them. We still made a good 35 miles a day with Patton's tanks (Worden).

The kinetic team membership was spontaneous. They did not know what they were doing, where they were going and probably had no idea who was really in charge beyond the man at the top and the one leading them at any given moment. They proceeded and continued to fight. Their group seems to have developed the ability to rapidly integrate and get focused on what needed to be done in order to survive.

The accelerated pace of decision-making, socialization and fighting for one's life gave rise to many exceptions to normal group behavior. Outsiders were German soldiers. Unit and membership in a specific part of the organization did not matter, so much as being another soldier to join in the fight. Time could sort out the details, but for the moment, survival was paramount.

We can take this observation as an important point because it illustrates that group leadership and individual leadership emerges in a crisis. In effect, unit cohesion is a by-product of the crisis. And, the leader who emerges in the crisis and takes control of the group successfully in such circumstances of spontaneity may do so for a brief time, as long as the crisis demands, and then due to the fluidity of the situation may fade back into the follower role. This is somewhat contrary to many views of military leaders, especially at the first line leader level, but these type of situations happened on several occasions throughout the accounts. Soldiers just rose to the occasion in certain circumstances, and when the situation called for an individual with a particular skill set, they simply acted without thinking of it in advance.

Spontaneous Group Actions in War

Theoretical Perspective

Northouse compares conditions of group effectiveness and characteristics of team excellence. The key aspects of the theories of Hackman & Walton (Conditions of Group Effectiveness, 1986), and

Larson & La Fasto (Characteristics of Team Excellence, 1989) are shown in the table below (Table 5). The spontaneous group leadership that appeared at D-Day and similar situations discussed in the accounts of the D-Day veterans show many parallels to both of these theories. Though the teams that we discuss were *ad hoc* in nature due to the fluidity of the battlefield, there existed the basic structural integrity, value system and hierarchical chain of command systems that aided in their formation and function. Larson & La Fasto's work focused on "what characterizes effectively functioning teams". They found eight characteristics common to team excellence. Though arrived at in a different way, Hackman & Walton suggested a theory of what criteria might be needed for goal accomplishment for teams. These criteria were *condition*-based. One can apply both models to interpret the observations from the D-Day Study. Table 5 presents a comparison of these two approaches.

Table 5. Comparison of Key Aspects of
Two Group and Team Performance Theories

CONDITIONS OF GROUP EFFECTIVENESS (Hackman & Walton, 1986)	CHARACTERISTICS OF TEAM EXCELLENCE (Larson & La Fasto, 1989)
Clear, engaging direction	Clear, elevating goal
Enabling structure	Results-driven structure
	Competent team members
	Unified commitment
	Collaborative climate
Enabling content	Standards of excellence
Expert Coaching	Principled leadership
Adequate material	External Support

(From Northouse, 2004)

In the case of the veterans from D-Day we can incorporate this model as part of the way to frame the spontaneous leadership that enabled teams to form and coalesce under varied circumstances during the campaign. An example of how these two models can be used based on the circumstances of the men in our study is shown below in Table 6.

Table 6. Application of Hackman and Walton Conditions and Larson and Le Fasto Characteristics to D-Day 60 Study Group

CONDITIONS OF GROUP EFFECTIVENESS (Hackman & Walton, 1986)	CHARACTERISTICS OF TEAM EXCELLENCE (Larson & La Fasto, 1989)	D-Day 60 STUDY GROUP
Clear, engaging direction	Clear, elevating goal	Assault Beaches
Enabling structure	Results-driven structure	Squad/PLT/CO Structure
	Competent team members	Officers/NCOs
	Unified commitment	Cause to free Europe
	Collaborative climate	
Enabling content	Standards of excellence	Military/national values
Expert Coaching	Principled leadership	Formal leadership/ Informal leaders
Adequate material	External Support	Initial/extensive organizational support of Allied Forces

The D-Day group we studied had all of the key components listed in both the group effectiveness model presented by Hackman and Walton and the team excellence model of Larson and LaFasto. The participants had a clear over arching goal, as well as an immediate one to assault the beaches or towns held by the Germans. They had a clear command structure and support system in place consisting of both officers who planned, and non-commissioned officers who were responsible for the training. They shared in a unified endeavor to free Europe, as well as common national values. These commonalities parallel the requirements of both group effectiveness and team excellence. Adequate material and external support were provided through the extensive organizational support of the Allied Forces. So, on a macro scale, the conditions had been established for success of the military. But the critical implementation of that success became a micro-scale event, where leadership and teams had to be effective at the squad, platoon and company levels as well.

The formal backdrop of the organization allowed informal teams to develop because the pre-existing values, command structure, and mutually supportive goals and jobs, allowed quick integration and synchronization.

Study Observations of Spontaneous Leadership

Several subjects talk about how the soldier or group of men with them acted in spontaneous ways that had nothing to do with the mission. C.K. Harris relates an occasion when his fellow soldiers were in Germany on patrol, and one of them had this idea:

> Somebody said "Let's go see if we can get a beer." A woman led us through to a special room in this place we were at. It turns out that it was the recently departed German commandant's lunchroom (Harris).

Harold McCauley and his fellow GIs took it a couple steps further after a few days of tough fighting on Omaha Beach. McCauley and his men rustled up some cattle, took over a German field kitchen and, just as typical of the American soldiers I served with Iraq, held a barbeque:

> Maybe I shouldn't tell this but it was our first invasion, and we knew there was cattle so this guy Lester Limbough from Winchester, Tennessee . . .

> Well, we captured the German kitchen . . . We got it brought up to the beach here and about the third night we had a heckle I mean there was cattle all over. We butchered out the hindquarters. Put on some English Channel salt water for

seasoning. And they had some onions with them, so we got some onions out of the gardens and maybe a few potatoes, they were small, and sea radishes, just loaded it. I mean you could have smelled it back in the United States. People kept coming in, engineers and such, different outfits . . . it lasted for about three days (McCauley).

Charles Shearer from the 439th TCG (Troop Carrier Group) was a glider pilot at Normandy. His glider carried Airborne troops to Normandy. Once he had discharged his cargo of paratroopers and had landed, the logical thing to do would be to evade the enemy and stay under cover, or head back to a rally point. However, he and his fellow crew members had a different idea:

We found a jeep and grouped up with some other guys but the jeep was damaged so we couldn't use it. We made our way back towards the beach and hooked up with some more guys, near to St. Mere Eglise. We made our way up a road and were invited into a bakery cafe for food and drinks. The family that ran the place was very glad to see us though they did not speak much English. There were many of us from my group at the table that night, and we ate a lot and drank even better! The wine was good enough to give me a terrific hang-over the next day. We took that moment to get know some of the folks we had come to liberate. The bakery owner kept bringing out that wine, and we kept toasting the liberation (Shearer).

Another account, showed how spontaneous leadership can occur in less threatening circumstances and can lead to high adventure. This recollection by Harry Brown, discusses how the opportunity to go on a quick reconnaissance adventure in Paris, despite a war going on around him, proved to be too much to resist for him and his companions. Brown was a replacement at the time assigned to the 2nd Engineer Combat Battalion. He and the mail handler, a man named Denwitty, and another soldier went AWOL to Paris during a lull in the fighting. They arrived there in advance of the other troops and joined in with French troops marching in the city on Bastille Day, before General De Gaulle arrived to liberate the city. Brown and his companions found time to visit the Arche de Triomphe and visit the place de Pigalle:

> We went AWOL to Paris, 3 of us. That was my big memory of WW2, one day in Paris. 24 hour day. I did all the usual things, almost, now don't get any ideas. (Laughter). I'm not going to tell you the truth. (Laughter) I got drunk. Marched in a parade. Kissed a bunch of girls, and got kissed by a bunch of girls. I think I did everything I was supposed to do. I survived.

> . . . make a note of this, this was before De Gaulle got here, we beat him, we beat him by a few weeks, there were still Germans around. Most of them were patients, recuperating, rehabs, not too many of them were, I did not see or hear or know of anyone firing a shot at me or anyone else, though they say they did. I wasn't listening for them. I was busy. There was no lights, and everything was dark. The subways were shut down, it was almost a dead town. We found a little restaurant that had some food yet, and we managed to eat while we weren't that hungry to tell you the truth. The next day . . . we went back to our outfits, by St. Lo and Paris, and we started moving again . . . See what happened was they were out of gas, there was no gas, so we had to wait there, and no one knows when it's going to get there and you know the army, you might be there for six months (Laughter). Well you know, anyway, we took the gamble, but we knew we'd better not try and stretch it (Brown).

**Allied soldiers marching in Paris on the Champs Elysee in late August 1944.
Corporal Harry Brown and friends made their way to the city weeks before it
was liberated in a moment of spontaneous group leadership.**
(Source: http://docs.fdrlibrary.marist.edu)

Corporal Brown's account of high adventure is not isolated. Many
veterans related similar tales. It is not surprising that such events
occurred. Based on the earlier discussion of some of the rebellious
tendencies of many leaders, this is typical. In Brown's instance, his unit
was part of the Allied forces that had run out of gas and were waiting
for supplies. In typical pragmatic American soldier fashion, he and his
buddies engaged in the most logical thing that came to their minds—a
road trip to Paris. The emergence of such traits of rebellion within a
group are not necessarily indicative of a lack of discipline but were more
the product of pragmatism by the soldier who finds himself caught in
a strange paradox of danger and safety, in an ethereal holding pattern
between violent savagery and boredom. Under such circumstances,
not knowing what lay in front of them but knowing what they had
already experienced, such behavior seems almost rational. Such accounts

of soldiers spontaneously acting as a group and establishing such parenthetical adventures in the middle of the anarchy of war have been the stuff of novels and tales as long as there have been wars. It is a part of the warrior ethos and culture, that even today, soldiers' experience. There are the official rules and regulations on what should be done, and most soldiers will follow these. But there are plenty of occasions when circumstances take on an entirely new dimension, and individuals or groups of soldiers will set up their own foxhole or sub-culture wherever they find themselves, whether for a day, a week or a year.

Other Aspects of Spontaneous Team Leadership

Several of the following accounts did not occur as part of the action at D-Day. However, as part of the general discussion on spontaneous leadership, I felt it appropriate to include several accounts of anecdotes from veterans describing events that occurred after D-Day or in some cases accounts of veterans who were not even at D-Day.

For example, SGT Frederick Carter of the British Royal Air Force was not at D-Day. But his accounts provided an outstanding example of spontaneous leadership that occurred in a different way. He was a prisoner of war in a camp where there were soldiers of many different nations, including Americans. In this recollection, Carter illustrates how even the difficult circumstances of being in a prison camp can have light moments, even while a group consciousness emerged. In their free time the men in the camp would play softball with American troops, and sometimes they played soccer or rugby. There were men in the camp who tried to escape as well. A Greek captain made wire cutters from ice skates. Others dug tunnels but were unsuccessful in escaping. Carter recalls some of the attempts and challenges faced by those who did. When asked if many people tried to escape, he responded:

> Oh yes. They had big tunnels and nobody got . . . we were on a peninsula and as soon as somebody escaped they just cut the peninsula. There were Americans there that spoke fluent German because they came from German families. They went out as Germans, but they didn't get very far. It was very difficult. I think in the whole war only two ever got out and

got back to England. If you got caught you got put in solitary. And I think the Greek captain was put in for about nine months because I think he was Jewish. He looked Jewish and they left him in there. They wouldn't let him out. Apart from that . . . (pause). Oh there were quite a few tunnels. They tried all sorts of things to get out (Carter).

Their sports matches were a pleasant diversion from the difficulties of being prisoners of war. Carter mentions this humorous anecdote:

We played cricket but we enjoyed softball. We used to pull the legs of Americans. Now you know what pulling a leg is. We played softball and suddenly someone would say, "Tea break!" And all the Brits would go sit off on a tea break. It infuriated the Americans. Here they are waiting in the field (laughs) . . . But they all took it in good fun. You had to do things otherwise life was a bit heartless . . . the only other thing that was really funny was once a month everyone had to go outside for their photographs and the Germans checked out. We were sort of next to the headquarters. And they put the boxes on the table when they finished. Well, we had an Irish squadron leader who was in charge of escape and that. When they weren't looking he {grabbed} a whole box of them, went indoors and put them in the fire you see. When they got back to their headquarters and they checked, there was a whole box missing. So everybody had to turn out. They had fifteen thousand people out in the field looking for them and we were pretending to dig up the sand and put them in. The Germans were shouting and pointing and they wrecked the whole field over it. But of course they were burnt, they weren't there (Carter).

Carter's recollection of various people taking on different leadership roles, even if it was small acts of defiance such as the Irish Squadron leader in this excerpt, or the Greek captain's escape attempts, shows how informal group structures can bring out leadership. The dynamics that are at work in such examples can take place over a short or long period of time. Additionally, this type of leadership is hinted at in the account given by a member of the French resistance, Pierre Collard. The resistance, or Maquis, had to work in small informal group structures scattered throughout France. They operated an informal network that combined former military and local citizens, who were mentioned in several accounts, particularly those of paratroopers who had landed off course.

Another example of spontaneous team leadership comes from the recollections of a former member of the French Resistance. Collard said he was in the Maquis, and as was noted earlier in the chronological review, the Maquis were not operating on D-Day, but operated further south. Nonetheless, Collard was a veteran, and his group's activity, as he so candidly points out, had an effect on the outcome of the Allied campaign. Collard's is the only resistance account in our study group, but shows a glimpse of the make-up and personality of such leaders. Collard was 93 years old at the time of his recollection. He said that the Maquis, who were a part of the French Resistance, was formed by former French soldiers when the Germans disbanded the Army. They sabotaged trains, roads, bridges, and conducted ambushes. They had regular contact from London through an American OSS (Office of Strategic Services) officer, as well as a couple of British officers and an Irish woman. Collard was proud of the role he and the resistance played in the War:

> I: So their activities helped the Americans here by delaying the Germans?
>
> C: Yes, our role in resistance was to either obligate them to deploy forces around us while we sought to regain the cities and regain control, or to disrupt and deplete the forces before they got to Normandy. General Eisenhower, in his book, My Crusade in Europe wrote that the work of the Maquis was equivalent to fifteen divisions.
>
> I: Did the American special team teach you about explosives?
>
> C: Yes, the French troops responded to a call to show up but they had nothing. They were trained and equipped by the American units. They had nothing but "balls" (courage) (Collard).

The French resistance movement was certainly an organization that had to function in strict trust and discipline, but also in extraordinarily informal ways. As Collard reports, the Resistance was made up of many former soldiers. These men had formal military training and could follow orders. Still, as Collard describes his unit's activities, it is clear that the type of leadership that emerged in this type of scenario did not follow the standard hierarchical organization chart. A large unit would have been discovered and its members killed by the German Army.

Other aspects of spontaneous leadership had a more negative side. This could be described as spontaneous lack of leadership. The following are two examples of this. In one case, CPL Walter Raymond discusses prisoner of war treatment and how a loss of accountability is suggested for some actions that may have taken place, the second is a tragic example of complete absence of leadership and its consequences, when a group of soldiers were nearing the end of their tour in Europe.

CPL Raymond was with the 79th INF Division. This was his account of how spontaneous leadership may have taken a different direction by the group setting aside its normal ethics code due to the circumstances of the fight. When asked how prisoners were treated by his squad, he replied:

> We didn't get too many prisoners, but when we got prisoners they went back. I'm not going to say (pause). I'm sure things happened because I've heard shots out there, you know. I don't know, but I'm sure (inaudible) you can almost (chuckles) take a gun and shoot. I'm sure it was done but like I say, what could you do (Raymond)?

Raymond all but says prisoners were shot with his knowledge. One cannot judge him or his fellow soldiers for what may have been done in today's lens. However, it suggests that such things were common and that the ethical values may have emanated from the group and been more fluid when the presence of stronger, more ethical leadership was not present.

One tragic case of what can occur when leadership is absent took place well after D-Day, when the war was nearly over. Though this did not happen at D-Day, it could just as well have occurred there as at any other time when a leader was absent. Similar to an earlier account of men playing football on the beach immediately after the invasion and a man was blown up by a piece of unexploded ordinance, in this account men were playing with a real bomb. Unfortunately, the group as whole seemed to have lost its common sense, perhaps due to the boredom of waiting for the end of their tour or perhaps because they had gone through so much that they had become numbed to the dangers that were still around them. Whatever the cause, there was a spontaneous lack of leadership that emerged, as their former company commander, Richard Burwash, recalls one tragic incident that occurred after the war in Europe was over and his men were staying in one of the cigarette camps. The camps were in France and were named after brands of cigarettes:

> How we lost two men was very tragic. While we were hanging around waiting for something to happen, we'd go up to the range and do a little shooting to get our qualifications up. I had set up a wire fence around this ammunition dump with bomb warning signs all around. We weren't that far from the range. We were just a bunch of kids and the war was over there. We got in a couple of trucks and one of my guys went over to the fence and because he had spotted a small canister on the fence line. He picked it up, and sure enough, it was a butterfly bomb with an instantaneous fuse.

> Well, this wasn't the bad part. He brings this thing back, and they start playing catch with the damn thing in a circle—11 guys in all. I would have blown my stack if I knew what they were doing. The guy who brought it from the fence ended up with it and put it between his legs for a moment. And this was not the bad part, either! This thing finally goes off, and kills two guys about five feet away, standing right in front of the guy who had it between his legs and to really seal the deal—he was not injured at all!

> The Germans dropped these things by the thousands all over the countryside. It was one of my jobs to find them and take them out of action. Losing two men on our way home was too hard to accept (Burwash).

Burwash's account has an especially tragic twist since they had not lost anyone during the fighting. It shows that leaders must remain vigilant and responsible until the job is completely done and everyone has made it home. It is indicative of what bored men who are used to danger and challenging situations can do once the pressure has let up. In the previous examples, we saw spontaneous group leadership taking hold in a crisis as recorded among our veterans' accounts. Many times this spontaneity, often unspoken but felt, was what made the critical difference in the many life and death situations they faced. But, it also had its negative side and shows how soldiers allowed mistakes to occur when they allowed the group to take over and lower itself to a lesser degree of thinking, as in this tragic case.

Comrades in Arms

Some of the most frequent examples of spontaneous leadership occurred among small groups of two or three. These accounts are particularly noteworthy, because leadership must surface when the pressure is on and there is no one else to make the decisions. Loyalty for a cause or unit is superseded by loyalty to one's battle buddy. The accounts that displayed these examples give pictures of when men were up against the wall, odds against them and somehow managed to survive as a team. Earlier, we presented an example of a reconnaissance team that had been sent by General Patton, one of several decoys that were deliberately sent to mislead the enemy. However, Norman Schein had another idea in mind:

> So we went out. At night we were to look around, and during the day time, we were to hide. Then one night we were driving, and . . . coming down a hill. I heard a terrible roar. There were no lights, of course, and I looked closely. It was a German convoy coming come up with Tiger tanks in it. My partner got excited: "What are we going to do?" We can't get out of here." When the tanks went by, they were going slow. They were about 40 yards apart, so I drove between two Tiger tanks. Then when I saw a road I could see clear enough, I drove out. That's how we got away from them, but they never knew we were there. My partner just about went crazy:

"You know what you just did?" I said, "Yeah, but we made it"
(Schein).

"Yeah, but we made it." Schein said to his buddy. It was a situation
that demanded an intrepid spirit, cool, calm nerve, courage and
leadership or it would all be over.

Another example of this type of leadership occurred in an account
given by SSG Paul Merriman. Although this happened six months after
D-Day, it is similar to Schein's account, as the men were well ahead of
their own lines and had to hide from the enemy. It was later in the war,
during the Battle of the Bulge. Merriman, along with two other men,
was on forward observer duty. The weather made flying impossible in the
Piper Cubs used at that time. The men were in their jeep with a radio
and were caught in a snow storm, away from their unit, surrounded by
the enemy and with dusk approaching they took shelter in some hidden
pine trees. They radioed to their headquarters and received this sage
advice, "Find someplace to hide!" The men looked for a foxhole and
fortunately found one that could accommodate three of them. Eight
inches of snow fell, according to Merriman, and in the morning their
jeep, affectionately called "Daisy Mae" {probably named for an attractive
female character in the "L'il Abner" comic strip about hillbillies}
was buried in snow and hidden in the pines, helping to prevent their
discovery by the Germans. The men kept radio silence and waited.
Merriman recalls that many American prisoners were taken during this
time, so he and his comrades stayed hidden in their foxhole:

> Our feet were a little cold, but it was better to have two guys
> around you than to be off by yourself. The next morning
> when we woke up, it had cleared and the Germans had gone,
> at least that's what we heard. We didn't see anyone at all.
> Lying on the ground were leaflets, and they were safe conduct
> leaflets. On one side it showed a picture of Lifesaver candies,
> which would get our attention, and on the other side was the
> safe conduct pass. It said to give yourself up, and you'll be
> accorded safe passage to the rear according to the articles of
> war and you will be well taken care of, and so on. Underneath
> in German it gave instructions to the captors (Merriman).

Certainly, the men were lucky to be alive, but they were also smart enough to stay put and must have worked together to get themselves hidden away from the Germans as they came through during the offensive that occurred around them. Fortune favors those who are smart enough to seize opportunities presented, and these men wasted little time in hiding. The snow provided an additional layer of cover for them. But ultimately, the small trio knew that if one of them was to break silence, run, or make any move that it would have been a death sentence for all of them. In short, they had their own group leadership surface in order to protect them and see them through the crisis.

Summary of Spontaneous Leadership Actions

Cases of spontaneous leadership occurring appear regularly throughout the accounts. We have presented examples of pairs and small groups of men almost automatically assuming or following both leadership and behavioral cues that were reactive to the environment around them. Much of this was informal and by many definitions might not have been classified as leadership because it resulted in tragic consequences or ignoring ethical norms. Yet, this behavior occurred and was practiced by the groups in much the same way as if they had been trained to know how to do it or follow such patterns. So, for better or worse, spontaneous leadership brought out something in the men that was not instilled there from training or directive. It was a bubbling to the surface of traits, good or bad, that were drawn out because of the circumstances.

Throughout this chapter we have observed several different manifestations of spontaneous leadership traits in groups. They are categorized below:

> Immediate and fluid group roles: Scattered men coming together to form *ad hoc* groups to react to situations, followed by different leaders surfacing and role changing

> Long term informal and inter-group roles: Prisoners of war interacting among their own groups and between groups (British/British, British-American) at the camp, all while

individually being free to follow their conscience with regards to escape attempts.

<u>Sudden informal leadership abdication</u>: Soldiers fooling around with a deadly bomb, or soldiers on patrol or in the fight ignoring ethical norms as a result of the stresses, group think, and overwhelming feelings of violence around them.

<u>Camaraderie leadership</u>: Groups of two or three where one member naturally asserted himself and took charge in an instance motivated to take care of his comrade and self, as in small recon teams sent out away from the main force.

<u>Instantaneous small group self-preservation</u>: When a group takes immediate action, with no dissent and little or no discussion in order to save itself.

The inference that can be drawn from these accounts is clear—leadership traits come to the surface when conditions require that to happen. Were it not for emergence of this leadership trait response or mechanism, many of the men, in these accounts and those with them would have faced a much greater challenge to survive, and in many cases may not have survived. The factors which cause this phenomenon to happen are more than simply bravery or self-preservation. The added dimension and synergy of the group, and the dynamics brought out in this environment calls for leadership, in one form or another, for better or for worse.

CHAPTER 8

TRAINING FOR D-DAY

Introduction

THE PREPARATION OF THE TROOPS for D-Day was a monumental task. Nearly every account referred to the training that was received in one form or another prior to the invasion. Most accounts presented the training in a positive manner, with few exceptions.

Types of Soldier Training for D-Day

D-Day training was given high marks by most accounts in a multitude of areas. The training given varied for each specialty; it was not simply drill and ceremony, marching, and marksmanship. The accounts give a vivid and realistic portrayal of what that training was like and how the men felt about it, both at the time, as well as years later. Although some accounts include some mistakes in place names, they certainly were more than adequate to give a geographic location and description of what the experience was like.

Most soldiers went through basic training, military occupational specialty training, and then were shipped over to England, mostly, for further training and exercises prior to the invasion. On the other hand, a good number of soldiers in our accounts received additional training or were in elite units such as the 101st and 82nd Airborne Divisions. At least 26 of the men interviewed were Airborne and two others were Rangers. Additionally, 16 of the 108 accounts used were from officers, many of them being former enlisted soldiers. Others had training that varied from linguistics training to high tech communications and avionics.

In addition to the training they received from the military, the men brought their own sets of skills with them. Jobs included boatbuilding, farming, lithography, clerical work, and trucking. Several were students who quit high school, others were in college. Their civilian work was not a large factor in their military jobs, but their life experiences did seem to play a role, particularly when discussing leadership experience preparation. One example of this was provided by David Roderick who joined the Army in 1940 at age 16. Roderick's parents were both dead. The circumstances of the Depression made for tough times. Roderick decided it would be better for the family if he went into the world and joined the Army. He was a natural athlete, and played all the typical sports of young Americans of his day: football, basketball, and baseball. He continued playing sports in both the military and later on in college. Roderick was in the 4th Infantry Division and he recalled his company commander this way:

> I was with the 22nd Infantry Regiment, 4th Infantry Division when we landed on Utah Beach on D-Day. My training was good, and my company commander was a West Point graduate, and a strict disciplinarian. He followed through with his West Point training to be sure that we were the best-trained as possible (Roderick).

We see in Roderick a way where his talents in team sports enabled him to adapt to the military, perhaps better than others of his generation who were drafted. The tough life of the Depression gave him few options, but he was fit and he had drive, so he went into the military, and after successfully completing his service, he even went on to college. He did not do too badly for a depression era kid who was on his own at 16. Roderick's military training was provided by the military, but by the time he reached Normandy, for him, and many others, life had already hardened and steeled his resolve for success. Roderick's leadership and drive seem to have emerged early because he was a team-player and was able to handle military life at a young age. While training certainly helped him, he must have had a lot of personal drive to have gotten as far as he had on his own. A trait such as this was not learned at D-Day, it was already inside him back in 1940. He had the raw material inside of him. However, he also notes the leadership of his commander, whose discipline also had an effect on him and helped him, either through example or task, to think beyond the present situation and look forward to college and graduation.

Before proceeding into more of the accounts, it would be helpful to point some of the background empirical data of the typical soldier of World War II, specifically in regards to the indoctrination and integration of the huge influx of "citizen soldiers" who almost overnight transformed the small professional pre-World War II Army into the one that showed up on the beaches of Normandy less than three years later. It was a remarkable transformation. The problem that faced the Army was how to train thousands of young recruits and turn them into soldiers in as little a time as possible:

> To return to the Army's problem of indoctrinating its leaders and its "led," we repeat that the critical problem was to mobilize informal pressures of the soldiers in support of their fellows who conformed and against the nonconformist, and to maximize the internalization of the controls through habituation. Moreover, unlike society at large, which has the entire period of childhood to mold the plastic youth into the image of a citizen, the Army had to move very fast indeed (Stouffer et al., 1949).

The basic training experience was more than simply molding the soldiers from external pressure of the formal training—it was a combination of many factors that came together and worked towards making the individual function as part of the larger organization. The purpose was not to create a mindless automaton, but a soldier who could in a short time function as a critical part of the team. The internal values of being a man, American, and peer pressure all played into this:

> The basic training period was, therefore, not one of gradual inculcation of the Army *mores,* but one of intensive shock treatment. The new recruit, a lone individual, is helplessly insecure in the bewildering newness and complexity of his environment. Also he is a man; he must show that he is tough enough to "take it." He is an American; the Army is a means to winning the war; he must do his best or lose face at home. With personal insecurity on the one hand, and the motivation to "see it through" on the other, he is malleable to the "discipline," which consists of a fatiguing physical ordeal and a continued repletion of facts until they become semi-automatic, in an atmosphere dominated by fear. As

one recruit put it, perhaps with exaggeration, "The recruit is warned and threatened, shouted at and sworn at, punished and promised further punishments with such frequency and from so many sides that he gets to gets to be like the rat in the neurosis production experiment. He soon comes to fear the Army and his superiors who represent it." The individual recruit is powerless. He finds solace in the company of his fellows, who are new and bewildered like himself, but who now, with all escapes blocked by fear of formal punishment, further each other's adjustment to the inevitable by applying sanctions of their own to those who "can't take it." The fear of being thought less than a man by one's buddies can be as powerful control factor as the fear of the guardhouse. When the former is socially directed to reinforce the latter, the Army has begun to succeed in building a soldier—a process which continues until as much as possible is internalized and automatized in the form of "conscience" (Stouffer et al., 1949).

Basic training was only one part of the challenge. The rest of the job was getting these men to fit into the units they were joining, often as fresh recruits who knew nothing of the informal rules and ways of doing business within the unit. For the leaders of these units, this was a significant problem. General Gavin's earlier mentioned strategy of keeping a strong cadre behind in England paid big dividends once the invasion started, as it helped keep a level of continuity in the organization. Overall, the problem of getting all of these men integrated into the ever expanding Army was a significant challenge, and the Stouffer study summed up what the empirical data showed:

The learning process was complicated by the fact that the formal rules, detailed and elaborate as they were, and embodying the past experience and long traditions of the regular Army, were progressively inundated by a flood of new and rapidly modified enactments required to meet the ever-changing situation presented by the rapid growth of the civilian Army and by the new demands of World War II.

Simultaneously, ever larger and larger proportions of both commissioned and non-commissioned officers comprised hastily trained civilians who could hardly have mastered all the old Regular Army rules and regulations, much less the new ones. Little wonder, under these circumstances, that the rules and regulations with which the bewildered recruit frequently found himself confronted were those improvised, remembered, or looked up for the occasion by the current commander, sometimes in support of his personal predilections or purposes. Irv Koplovitz gives an account that was typical of the training many of the soldiers who went to Normandy experienced in their preparation for the invasion. Koplovitz went to basic training, and then more specialized training, that was to ready him for his role in the invasion:

> I was drafted into the service in July, 1942. After basic training at Atlantic City, New Jersey, I went to Ft. Logan, Colorado mainly to be trained for engineering and operations. I was then assigned to a troop carrier command and I went to Louisville, Kentucky for more training, then I was sent to Texas. I was a private during this training period. I worked in an office that was mostly orderly procedure stuff. Once guys got in, and made it through basic training—and it didn't matter if they were drafted of volunteered—they were all the same. They knew what to expect.

> In the 30 days I had all this training, I learned more during that time than four years of college when it came to handling the paperwork needs of the troops. My biggest effort came when soldiers got their pay and letters from home. Having both of these things done on time was a big morale booster for the troops. I was always taught that if you have a group of men that are happy and content with their jobs, you will have a good outfit, and that's exactly what we were (Koplovitz).

Another example of how the training prior to D-Day was conducted is given by the 9th ID's John Johnson, a former boat builder turned infantry soldier:

> I: What sort of training did you get?

> J: Infantry training.

I: Did that prepare you for what you needed to do later?

J: It certainly did. For ten weeks of hard training. Infantry training.
We landed first in Glasgow and de-boated in Balfran (?) and trained (took a train) to England to a tent camp.

I: So you were then in a tent camp in England?

J: That's right . . . I don't know the name of the town. It was a small place.

I: What sort of training did you do in England then?

J: We did briefings and that sort of thing to keep us busy. We had dry runs . . . at camp.

I: What did they consist of?

J: On D-day we were ready to go. It's a dry run, don't go back to get the tents . . . and finally one day it happened. (Johnson).

Johnson's account does not refer much to the appearance of traits, but it nonetheless describes the process the soldiers went through. This process added a level of confidence and competency in the tasks they would be called upon to perform when they hit combat. The relationship to leadership and traits drawn from this and other similar accounts is that the training served as a way to unlock the traits that were in the solider, to get him comfortable with leading actions, and to spur development of leaders who were already in place. In Johnson's case, this training paid big dividends, not in his own actions, but in the actions of those who saved him after he was wounded:

I: Sir, what would be your most vivid memory of the war?

J: I think that the thing that impressed me the most was the way I was evacuated after I was wounded. The medics got to me right away and two of them took me out on my rifle just like we were trained to and the medics and the hospital staff at the field hospital made me so comfortable. That stood out (Johnson).

Another perspective comes from Lieutenant Frederick Crispin, who served as a navigator in a C47 that carried troops over to the drop zone on D-Day. When asked about any parting comments on the overall experience, he stated:

We were so well-trained and so well provided for that after the war I realized the support we had. During the war I didn't realize it, but all of those tires, and brakes, and gears, and gliders had to come from somewhere. [laughs] I didn't realize it at the time. The only thing I knew was that we had brought our own plane over (Crispin).

The training was all part of a larger effort, an effort that went far beyond the training he had received. The British Navy's Henry Roy Chilton described his training this way:

There was a lot involved with the training for us in 1943. We were trained with rifles and basic seamanship. It was hard training. I went from basic training to another base where the Royal Marines were trained near the coast by the River Thames. I was put into combined operations.

We trained right up to the time of D-Day. I felt there was something important on the cards as we were moved around the country to various places. I think we all knew that this training was all about something big (Chilton).

Nearly all the men in the study reported they felt a sense of importance in the training prior to the invasion. Chilton's comments reflect this. This may have added to their focus as they got closer to the actual event.

Carl Cannon was a soldier from the 4th Infantry Division. He was not drafted, but instead enlisted in 1940 and was a seasoned veteran by June, 1944:

I enlisted in March of 1940. We didn't have basic training in a traditional sense then—we had individual unit training. I was in the 8th Infantry Division when we went to maneuvers in Louisiana {Editor's note: The Louisiana Maneuvers was a massive field exercise in Louisiana involving thousands of soldiers.}, then back to Fort Benning when we joined the 4th Infantry Division, which was forming at the time.

I was still at Fort Benning when Pearl Harbor happened. I would say the training was "good exercise" and after North Africa we developed more special training to adapt to the way the war was going. Anyways, we moved to Camp Gordon Georgia for more training before we went to Europe. The way we trained depended on which enemy we were going to face. We trained in Florida on the West coast near Tampa for our beach training. We trained on LCD's on the east coast of Florida and trained on shore landings.

We went to New Jersey, and took an old British ship to Liverpool, England, and began intense training near Exeter. We were training three times a week, sometimes overnight. They would move us to camps where they kept us under wraps and none of us could go anywhere (Cannon).

Richard Harrison was a member of the 82nd Airborne Division. He summed up the impact of his training experience and what it brought out in him with this statement:

After awhile, we felt like our 'number' was up, but I think I did a fairly good job while I was there. All the hardships made me much better as a man, and I must add that my training at Fort Benning was excellent. It prepared me for the job I had to do in Europe, to never "quit" at anything, and that stayed with me all my life (Harrison).

Harrison's take away from the experience was to "never 'quit' at anything", something that he felt was directly related to the tough training he received at Fort Benning. This helped him and many others succeed in the Army and the challenges they faced at Normandy. The training was varied, and opportunities to emerge as a leader presented themselves in many ways to all the men in the accounts. More training may have added to their focus as they got closer to the actual invasion itself. Additionally, because of all of the additional interest and effort placed on the units, soldiers, and new systems, it is likely that they also experienced what is described as the Hawthorne Effect (Landsberger, 1955): a higher output in performance because of the type of environment and feelings of competence to do their work (mission). These men received a lot of interest and special training. They believed in what they were doing, especially those in elite units, in terms of the training. As we transition to that aspect of training, we will see that the attention and challenge of such units brought together a tougher, smarter, group of men, whose commitment and bravery were tested long before they ever got on board a transport to England.

"I wanna be an Airborne Soldier . . ."

The title of this section is part of the refrain from a typical airborne cadence sung for the last sixty-plus years. Many of the men at D-day were sky soldiers, and their accounts from Sainte-Mère-Église and Sainte Marie du Mont have been listed throughout this discussion. These men were in units that were elite for their time, and that continue to be elite today. For those soldiers who had the drive to excel and the courage to do so, there was Airborne, Ranger, and other challenging specialty training. In 1944, being Airborne was still a very new and scary proposition. Consider that air flight itself was barely over a quarter century old. Add the prospect of jumping out of a perfectly good airplane into a field where people are shooting at you, and the picture is darker still. Yet, for the Airborne soldiers, there was a pride and dignity that took a stronger hold on its members than the fear. Men like Ridgway and Gavin recognized the need for such units to have more *esprit de corps* and higher standards, so that men who were motivated for a higher purpose would be proud to be part of that unit. In the study conducted by Stouffer and the War Department in 1949, this issue was examined. Additionally, this is a further indication of the Hawthorne Effect written about by Elton Mayo in his observations from work studies in the 1920's. Although drill and ceremony can be repetitive and monotonous, soldiering goes far beyond this, especially for Airborne soldiers and Rangers.

Did training play a role in this, or was there something more? To understand this, we need to understand a little bit of the background of why some men chose to even become members of parachute units. Part of the drive and motivation for being part of such units may have come from a desire to distinguish oneself from being simply another member who was out doing his duty just by being part of the machine. According to *The American Soldier, Volume II*, by Stouffer and colleagues (1949), by World War II, the distinction between combat soldier and non-combat soldier was sharper, while at the same time, society was not so judgmental if one had not been in combat, so long as one had at least shared in the burdens of serving the country in war. There was an expectation of service, but Stouffer notes a marked shift in societal mores from those of World War I. One passage from the Stouffer book highlights some of the aspects of this societal shift:

> In World War II there was much less community pressure on the young man to get into the Army. There were few real counterparts to the white feather, painting homes yellow, use of the epithet "slacker." The general attitude was that everyone should do what he was assigned as well as he could, but it was *not* considered essential that the individual "stick his neck out." To over-simplify, it might be said that in World War II, the test of social manhood began much farther from actual fighting than in World War I. In the First World War, a man was more severely censured for failing to enter the armed forces; this time, the test was more nearly whether he adequately filled his role once placed in the combat situation.

> Combat posed a challenge for a man to prove himself to himself and others. Combat was a dare. One never knew for sure that he could take it until he had demonstrated that he could. Most soldiers facing the prospect of combat service had to deal with a heavy charge of anticipatory anxiety. The more they heard about how tough the fighting was, the greater the anxiety and the insecurity that came from doubt as to whether they could handle the anxiety. Thus, combat might actually

come almost as a relief—it joined the issue and broke the strain of doubt and waiting (Stouffer et al.).

Airborne training and other training like it played a vital role in satisfying the desire for adventure and warrior spirit that had, according to this study, diminished throughout much of society by the early 1940s. The warrior spirit of these men was not satisfied with clerking or KP duty, and so they looked for opportunities to step out and become something more. This explains some of the reasons why many of the men in our accounts voluntarily underwent extremely rigorous and dangerous training, just to get the chance to be the first in, either by scaling a cliff to get shot at or by dropping from the sky and getting shot at. Either way, it took a lot of raw courage, determination, and leadership to get to such a point. The following accounts give a picture of the training these men endured, as well as how they responded to it. For example, Frank Bilich enlisted in the Army a week after he graduated high school. Despite flat feet and a heart murmur, Bilich not only completed the standard training, he even went on to jump training. His sergeant, nicknamed Flash Gordon after the serial film hero, led by example:

> There was a sergeant we called *"Flash Gordon"* who could really do anything. If he told us to run five miles, he would do those five miles with us. At the end of jump training, we all knew what we had to do. While I was in paratrooper training, my mother had run into a woman in a store whose son was with me and found out that I had joined the paratroopers. Of course, this wasn't part of what she had envisioned when I originally joined the infantry and she called the Chaplain at Fort Benning and arranged to meet with me. She took a train from Chicago all the way to Georgia to try and talk me out of staying with the paratroop regiment but there was no way I was going to give up (Bilich).

Bilich disregarded his own congenital frailties and his mom's entreaties to avoid such dangerous duty, and made his way into Airborne history. Fellow Division member Francis Lamoureux recalls the training even more vividly:

Intensive training, training, training, all the time. But that training at McCall was fantastic, that's where I got really know what kind of man Colonel Mendez was. [18] He would run our ass off. He would run us until we'd drop. When you see that guy ahead of you and he doesn't drop, you've got to keep up. Of course that first week at jump school, if you don't survive that first week you're out, they don't want paratroopers that cannot hold on, so they really put us through the ropes. The Marines can brag about what tough training they got, but I think we got a damn tough training down there when we were at Fort Benning in paratroop school just that one week there. Different stages, you've got first stage, second, third, fourth stages of it, but that first week was like hell, they put you through hell, obstacle courses, ju jitsu, you'd get so, at the end of the day you'd be luck to climb up and throw yourself on the bunk. The next morning every muscle in your body is stiff and you try and go down the stairs and you're crippled and think how am I going to survive another day of this . . . but then by the end of the week, you've got it made.

Lamoureux completed training at the Airborne school in Fort Benning. This training was followed by training at Camp McCall, where Lamoureux participated in exercises that went on regardless of the weather:

. . . those exercises took you out in the woods in the rain and lightning. Guys were being killed by lightning. We'd have little battles and skirmishes, we'd go out with water, with just a canteen, and spend a whole day out and come back and you had to have a canteen left, and if you didn't you were in trouble. Go get some pushups. Yeah, they put us through the test at McCall (Lamoureux).

---

[18] Lieutenant Colonel Louis Gonzaga Mendez, Jr. was awarded the Distinguished Service Cross for his actions during combat in World War II (Zabecki, 2009).

Another 82nd soldier who went through the tough training that was typical of the Division was Duke Boswell. His summation of the training is wrapped up in this statement:

> The training we got before the invasion was the most important part of our success, I think. Having enough ammunition was the next thing along with watching each other's backs all the time. We knew that the awareness of the man next to you might be the difference between life and death for everyone on the team.
>
> We—the airborne soldiers had done so well in our missions that the ground commanders requested us to join their forces often. We were always moving, and always fighting (Boswell).

Duke Boswell said that the training he received as an Airborne Soldier prior to the invasion gave him a confidence in his ability to do his mission, and, more importantly, it helped him develop a trust in the men on his team. One explanation of this would be that the training was a catalyst for bringing out bonding traits that helped cement the group response. Thus, the application of stress prior to the invasion resulted in better performance of the men when they reached combat, at least according to their points of view.

This gives further support to the premise that leadership traits emerge in a crisis atmosphere, real or perceived, or under battle stress, and are part of the internal make up of most people as a survival mechanism.

Bilich, Lamoureux, and Boswell all had tough training prior to D-Day. They were mentally tested, physically challenged to their limits, and subjected to restrictions that at times were almost prison-like. Tucker and Cannon both described humble backgrounds and had entered the Army prior to the Japanese bombing of Pearl Harbor. All three men had to have passed tough challenges just to become Airborne soldiers. However, the challenge to get into the unit, and that they overcame that challenge, leads to the observation that training was what catalyzed their leadership abilities, just as was reported in the conclusions of the empirical data in the Army Study. A good measure of the success of the training was the fact that these men survived D-Day and the war, and they were leaders in their own right, in separate units. Thus, the organizational training effect should not be discounted as a factor in leadership and the emergence of trait leadership in a crisis.

It is important to note, that it seemed to be more the triggering action of what was already within rather than something that they got because of the particular training.

This is an important point. Training is important and necessary, but the individual has, as has been shown throughout the accounts, a certain level of innate ability. It seems that the training brings out what is already there in the soldier, but training does not place the ability in the individual. This is an important distinction which sheds light on training and its purpose and value for developing leaders. Good training will bring out good leaders, but it will not bring all leadership traits to the surface. Different training experiences will trigger different traits at different times, and this is also contingent on the readiness and maturity of the individual.

Integration and training of new soldiers

A critical job of a leader is to ensure continuity within the organization. In combat, this became a monumental task. The leader had to take care of his soldiers who were already trained veterans, as well as had the additional task of getting replacement troops ready to fight and do their mission. Leaders who displayed concern for their soldiers and took the time to train the recruits were also taking time away from their own rest or recovery, putting themselves at risk. They had to rely on the courage of untested soldiers, and were forced to carry a heavier burden of responsibility in addition to the actual job training that had to be done.

The leadership traits required to lead a team and integrate new members into it included maturity, communication skills, and intelligence, as well as a level of compassion and understanding that allowed them to sense what needed to be done to get the individual soldier up to a level of confidence to function in combat. This was no easy task. Many men were suspicious of the untried green soldiers. Those who succeeded in this task were indeed special men. The United States Army calls the non-commissioned officer the backbone of the organization. The accounts from non-commissioned officers in the study demonstrate this in many ways. The men from our study who were charged with this training and leading these soldiers were from all types of units. The things they had in common were a sense of responsibility and the intrinsic motivation to look out for their troops, in this case, rookies.

Don L. Dicks was a member of the 82nd Airborne Division's 508th Parachute Infantry Regiment. He took his role as squad leader seriously and watched out for the new men:

> On D-Day I was a squad leader in the 1st platoon, Co. "I", 508th Parachute Infantry Regiment, 82d Airborne Division. We had basic infantry training in the states and after the Tennessee maneuvers in '43 we came over to Ireland and trained there for about 30 days while they was getting our tent city ready in England.
>
> The Normandy peninsula was our last big go around. We went back to England and got our replacements, and went through some training. I tried to match recruits up with what I call "regulars" when they first come to our unit, always with a fellow who had experience and so I told the young men, "You listen to what he tells you and do what he tells you and he'll train you (Dicks).

The wisdom from more than 60 years in the past is as relevant today as it was then. Dicks did not lead from reading a manual or listening to a focus group. He told his men what they needed to do and what they needed to know. He used a typical Army approach by making sure each newcomer had a battle buddy to learn from and keep him out of trouble. He followed his instincts and took care of his squad.

The use of veterans to train new troops was hardly a new idea. It was part of the integration plan for maintaining the 82nd Airborne Division's unit continuity, and it was applied in many different ways in other organizations as well. For example, Clifford Goodall, a Navy Signalmen recalls his experience of being shipped from the Atlantic theater to the Pacific theater in anticipation of the Invasion of Japan:

This was probably around September, but I had been over in England since January of 1944. They said we need all you guys with the supposed experience out on the west coast so that you can train these other sailors for the invasion of Japan . . . . I got out there and spent about three months doing absolutely nothing (Goodall).

Fortunately for Goodall he did not have to participate in the invasion of Japan, as the war ended before that became necessary. Nevertheless, he and many others, Army, Navy, or otherwise, were sent in large numbers back to the States and the West Coast to prepare for it. Many accounts in the study make reference to this, indicating that the men who served at D-Day were not only survivors; but also leaders and trainers whose knowledge and experience on the battlefield and carrying out operations was seen as a critical skill.

This review has shown that the experiences in training and integration from the veteran's accounts gives weight to the theory that leadership traits surfaced under the stressful, event-packed conditions of D-Day, and other similar experiences. It shows that integration played an important part in triggering this behavior for the role of the leader, as well as in creating the conditions for the integrating soldiers to have their own leadership traits emerge as they became part of the team.

Other training

Airborne and elite unit training was not the only training that was a priority for the invasion. Other training required men with certain skill sets and traits that were not common to all soldiers. One example of this critical training was in intelligence gathering. Arnold C. Franco, the radio message interceptor for the Air Force, had parts of his account introduced earlier in this work. His skill sets were not in hand-to-hand combat, but nonetheless he had to perform as a leader and execute missions that were critical to the effort. He was smart, mature, responsible, and dependable, with a strong work ethic. One had to have these qualities in order to do the mission he was called to do. Franco describes the process of training, and how he and the team he was on stepped up their performance as the mission became real time. He and nine other men were first trained at Michigan State University in German. This was followed by training at Vint Hill Farms in Warrenton, Virginia at a signal intelligence center. The men joined a newly formed organization called the 3rd Radio Squadron Mobile G (for Germany). It was a part of the Ninth Air Force. The Air Force's job was to win the Air War in Europe. Franco and his men played a crucial role monitoring transmissions of the German Luftwaffe:

> It was given extreme priority. The job was to monitor the German Air Force, the Luftwaffe, and it had several sections. One was what we called the Voice Intercept—people who were listening to German pilots talking. Others, like me were trained in Code Breaking; we listened to German radio messages, which came from German aircraft talking to German Ground stations. The third section was called Direction Finding; their job was to pinpoint those aircraft that we were listening to and find out their direction so they could be intercepted by allied fighter aircraft (Franco).

Franco's work was top secret. Many documents about it were never released to the public until years later. One was released as late as 1996. Franco wrote a book about his work called *Code to Victory*, as told to Aselin Spellman. Franco's efforts were noted by the British Commander who trained them:

> Well the British who trained us, [and] the Commander of that group, who turned out to be a very famous man—Group Captain Scott-Farnie. In October '44, four months after the invasion, he wrote a memo to SHAFE saying that we were the most effective mobile unit on the continent. So our teachers . . . in effect, we outdid our teachers (Franco).

The training Franco received was very specific and required a person with special talents. Others received training in one area and then found themselves doing a completely different job. But the important thing was what the training evoked in the individual. Frank Bilich, who was mentioned earlier, was a Croatian immigrant from Chicago. He joined the Army and earned his paratrooper wings serving with the 82nd Airborne. He described how he received one type of training but ended up doing another job. His account shows a combination of several themes that have been already discussed: mentorship and loyalty from his First Sergeant, trust in the men around him, and confidence in his mission and his cause. Overall, he sums up what the purpose of all that training was about: to be able to trust the men around him as they performed their mission together:

> When I joined the 505th in Northern Ireland, I sounded off my name and the First Sergeant asked to see me after the formation. It turns out he was my next door neighbor in Chicago who I used to play softball with when we were kids. He told me to pay attention to everything or that I wouldn't make it home. Having my old neighbor with me made things a lot easier for me.

> The Army trains you for one thing but you end up doing another. I was trained for demolitions but ended up with a radio, which I only used one time during the entire war.

> The jump into Normandy was the easy part. It was what happened every minute after the landing that made everything scary . . . . My first experience in combat was about ten o'clock that morning. We were walking up a road and some Germans opened up on us. We scattered in all directions until some of our guys knocked them down and we were on our way.

> I was perfectly at ease in the battles we fought because the guy on my left and the guy on my right was the best that could be and I could trust my life to them. We had a job to do, and we didn't question it. I knew we were all family and we still are today. (Bilich)

Franco, Bilich, and countless others trained to do one job and did another, but ultimately they were all soldiers. They all went to D-Day and did their duty and were ready for the leadership within them to emerge when the circumstances and events called for it.

Tragedy in Training

Training exercises were often dangerous. One exercise was operation Tiger. It took place at a training beach off the coast of southern England called Slapton Sands. It was a training disaster of such magnitude that survivors or men involved had to be kept separate from the rest of the soldiers and sworn to secrecy so that word would not get out and affect morale, or perhaps overall public opinion, so great was the scale of the loss of life due to enemy activity, security breaches, and failure of leaders and equipment. The Allied plan was to use this area as a warm-up for D-Day because it allowed them to replicate many of the conditions that the invasion force would be facing in Normandy. Unfortunately, the training had some terrible twists that more than replicated the conditions, and it turned from a training exercise into a tragedy that resulted in the depths of nearly 1,000 men.

The event at Slapton Sands was a test of not only the mettle of the soldiers who trained there, but also of the commanders and the leaders who planned it, and who had to live with the consequences of the event. It was to be a large-scale exercise to prepare for the invasion. Unfortunately, things went very wrong. The D-Day veterans provide the details about what happened. We can see from their accounts what traits surfaced under the stress of that event, how leaders acted, and how their followers, the men who recalled the events and experienced it acted and reacted. Despite the training tragedy, leaders at all levels had the opportunity to experience the combined effects of running multi-phased operations. Irv Smolens, of the 4th Infantry Division, discussed Operation Tiger in his account. He said that although it had tragic results, it served an important role in preparing for the Normandy Invasion, and that without the lessons learned from it the invasion would not have been as successful. But there was a high price. This idea was to be tested on Slapton Sands in *"Operation Tiger"*:

> We completed our part of the practice invasion and returned to our billets. Later on that evening, the support units were attacked by German E-Boats, like our PT boats on the water, sinking two LST's and almost 1000 Army, Navy and Coast Guardsmen were killed during that afternoon.

The local fishermen were complaining for years after the war that their nets were being caught there all the time. So, they sent a diver down and they found a Sherman Tank on the bottom. It was a secret operation and the families were not notified until after D-Day that their loved ones had died. Ike made sure that every one of the bodies was recovered because some of the officers had the D-Day invasion plans on them when they were really killed, which was April of 1944.

To me, this was the biggest part of the D-Day story. Without exercises like the one at Slapton Sands, the invasion would never have been the success that it was (Smolens).

Harold F. McCauley was a 4th Infantry Division DUKW operator at D-Day. His abbreviated account describes his background in the war prior to D-Day. McCauley's account of Slapton Sands was partially presented in the Chronology Chapter. The account we examine in this section gives more detail about the event and specifically how the mistakes by commanders impacted the soldiers only weeks prior to the invasion. He gives details of the formation of the unit and, specifically, he gives a perspective of Slapton Sands that does not gloss over what happened. McCauley was a veteran of several invasions (North Africa, Italy) by the time he reached Utah Beach. His unit was the first amphibious truck company formed, and saw action in North Africa, Sicily, and Normandy. Yet, Slapton Sands stood out from all of this and left an indelible imprint on him. His account is lengthy, but it gives a vivid portrayal of the life of what the men and the organization faced with the challenge of participating in an invasion. Additionally, it shows the breadth of interaction between leaders and average soldiers, as McCauley discusses how he met Eisenhower and was at many of the briefings prior to the invasion. McCauley, although separated many degrees by rank from his commander, nevertheless shared many experiences with him. McCauley describes his experiences below. His account not only describes Slapton Sands, but also the ordinary, mundane details of average soldiers in the war. His first action was in England and Ireland where they trained and then went on to North Africa where the Allied forces fought the French Legion until they joined the allies:

M: At that time there was no amphibious DUKWs. And we were still part of the 1ˢᵗ Engineer Amphibious Special Brigade. It was kind of a hand-picked bunch. We fought the French Foreign Legion for nine days. We got the first five DUKWs in Africa and we changed the name to 479th Amphibious Truck Company.

I: Okay, you want to explain what a DUKW is . . .

M: It was a G.I. truck made into a boat. Eighty percent of the parts were interchangeable. There was thirty, I would have said thirty-one but they say thirty-two in the book now . . . They were seven feet high and you had to crawl up the side of them to get in and jump out of them. And if you were getting bombed you would come out in a hurry . . . We hauled 40,000 casualties off of this beach{Editor's note: Utah Beach}, and the DUKWs never quit going for 120 days . . . [19]

I: They made life easier for landings?

M: Well we never had a port, everything that was taken in from in Sicily was hauled in by our company, 200 men and every wounded and every prisoner hauled out was by our company in Sicily.

We thought we were going home . . . they said they were going to train guys to go into France and it didn't quite work that way. I was on that exercise tiger lock [Editor's note: Exercise Tiger] invasion.

I: Okay, where was that.

M: In the sands where we landed back in. We was never briefed until that night, and maybe I shouldn't say this but . . .

---

[19] Editors Note: 4ᵗʰ Infantry Division was at Utah Beach. McCauley is most likely referring to his unit, and not simply his own DUKW's for which he was responsible.

were supposed to have been guarding our convoy. At 4:00
there were no escorts out there. Not an escort. The British
took off . . . we was doing with no protection, and about
midnight they opened the ramps and told me to hit, it will
be England, we didn't know whether we was going to land in
France or England. And there was a tube with a blue light in
it that was two feet across. And I must have been out trying to
follow the ships . . . they must have sank the ship that I was
on a few minutes after I got off (McCauley).

McCauley was in charge of three DUKWs. In his account he
discusses some of the events that he and his comrades faced together. For
example, he had a fight with one man who ended up becoming one of
his best friends:

One guy was an engineer and had been in every outfit in
the Army. He ended up in our outfit because there was only
one place worse than our company, and that was Dyers.
If we couldn't handle them they went to Dyers. This guy
had been an engineer and I got into a fight even. I was, he
said something to me and I broke his nose. (Laughter) He
shouldn't have said it and he broke my nose, we fought for
twenty minutes. It ended up the best fight that any two men
ever fought. (talking about after the fight) (McCauley).

McCauley finished his account by going to back to the Slapton Sands
event again. As mentioned in the Chronology, McCauley and his friend
Dwight Coles went out and picked up the floating bodies of men in the
water afterwards. He describes bodies being bulldozed over and he and
his men on lock down for the last weeks prior to the invasion. He also
describes the briefings, and despite the tragedy of Slapton Sands, shows
how both leaders and followers kept going and readying themselves for
the invasion of Normandy:

A few guys got out . . . The 478th Amphibious Truck
Company had taken cavalry in England out of our company
to form and they didn't have enough men to have roll call
when we got back . . . they were keeping us quiet so they put

us in barbed wire for fourteen days with guards on us. Seven men per tent and I can't tell you where it was in England but . . . about every two or three days we'd get briefed by Eisenhower and Montgomery . . . (McCauley).

McCauley's account gives a human touch to the event. Although he wanders a bit with his recollection, it actually gives more substance to the total experience of the typical soldier and leader of his day. One example of this was when as a leader he had to deal with a subordinate who was out of line. He directly confronted the man. There was a fight, certainly an unorthodox method in modern leadership conflict resolution, but in the end it resolved the issue. As an experienced leader, he was able to deal with the tragic loss of lives at Slapton Sands and continued to search for soldiers who had been lost in the water. As a leader, he kept what he knew secret for forty years. It was a burden for him to carry, and he was not alone. He mentioned that a general committed suicide over what had happened. It was in fact Rear Admiral Donald P. Moon's suicide that was attributed in part to the Slapton Sands incident (Yung). McCauley was fortunate to have survived. History records two major blunders at Slapton Sands: the lack of the protection for the LSTs by the Naval Forces, which enabled the German E-Boats to attack the LSTs, and the live fire that mowed down soldiers as they hit the beaches of South Devon, England. The other issue was that the flotation devices caused men to float upside down. (This was not only bad engineering and design, but also poor training for the hundreds of men who ended up drowning both at Slapton Sands, and again at D-Day, as has been mentioned in other accounts). McCauley also describes how he reached a culminating point about burying the dead after Slapton Sands. He is referring to information about the event. But underlying this is the fact that he lost a lot of faith and confidence in the overall leadership around him. On the other hand, he still supported his chain of command and did his duty, displaying loyalty and discipline. He searched for lost comrades, again showing loyalty and courage, as he and others fished men from the water instead of simply leaving them there, despite the dangerous waters and being overwhelmed by the unexpected loss of their comrades. He and the others who survived the event had to have a high level resiliency in order to bounce back and then go on to do the mission at D-Day only a few weeks later. Lastly, they were prepared for tough training, but they were not expecting to deal with a tragedy of this sort to occur, basically under the very eyes of their leaders at a training event.

Summary of Training Observations

The accounts of the study demonstrate that training played an important role in energizing and bringing to the surface the myriad traits that were requisite for successful leaders. Clearly there was a link between success on the battlefield and training before the event. The more challenging and realistic the training, the better prepared the leaders were when they reached Normandy. However, it also shows that the men all had to have a certain level of raw material of their own—traits—which enabled them to pass the tests and challenges set out before them. Lastly, the tragic events at Slapton Sands show that although tough realistic training plays an important role as a catalyst in developing leaders and preparing soldiers for training, it can come at a high cost, and senior leaders have to weigh this when making plans for large scale exercises which require close coordination between several organizations.

CHAPTER 9

WHY THEY DID IT

ONE QUESTION WHICH IS RELATED to the study of the leadership at D-Day and Normandy is why did they do it? Private Will Reagan was in the first wave of soldiers who landed at Omaha beach. He gives a vivid portrayal of landing at Omaha beach at 0630 on the 6th of June 1944:

> Well, there was thirty-six of us in an LCS, I think it was called. Two jeeps and two trailers loaded with TNT. Our objective was to go into their 483rd Red Dog. No, Dog Red beach . . . And clear a way for the infantry and the tanks and the trucks to come in behind us. Fighting was very heavy . . . . And we were caught in crossfire and we lost quite a bit of our, quite a few of our company. I was one of the fortunate ones that made it up to this point here. I think our objective was to get to a little town by the name of Saint Lo. No, Saint Laurent. Saint Lo is later. Saint Laurent was up on top . . . and our objective was to get there by noon and I don't think we made it 'til around three o'clock when the tanks got rolling (Reagan).

Reagan recalls how a fellow soldier was concerned about being charged for a radio that was damaged by enemy fire. Reagan himself describes how he was so occupied with trying to stay alive and get off the beach that he did not really have time to think and actually process the idea of the invasion not being successful. For Reagan and thousands of others like him, all that mattered was getting off of that beach alive:

> I: What do you remember about first hitting the beach? About actually . . . .
>
> R: Scared. Scared. Very scared, but then after we got going just means that you have to keep going or you were going to die there on the beach.

I: Yeah, was the gunfire . . .

R: MVA's, MVA's, artillery, (inaudible) guns, and machine guns. Heavy, very heavy. [20]

I: Did you lose a lot of equipment?

R: Someone in my company came up to me and he says "My radio doesn't work". I looked at him and it, looked like Swiss cheese. I said throw the damn thing away, it's no good anymore or it's not good to you, not good to anybody else. Doesn't even work. He says "I don't want to pay for it." I said you never have to pay for it. And he says . . . "My radio's not working. It looks like Swiss cheese." . . . . I'd say out of the thirty-six in the platoon, we lost about twenty men that day.

I: Twenty men . . . so it was fifty percent?

R: Right.

I: And how long did it take you to move up the beach, under the firing?

R: I want to say two hours but I'm not really sure . . . You know, I wasn't really timing it. So it's hard for me to remember really.

I: Were you just ducking behind whatever was around.

R: Hiding and running to keep going.

I: Yeah.

R: 'Cause all of us were scared, this was our first time in combat. Well, kind of.

---

[20]   Military Vehicle - Armored

I: Was there, was there a feeling that the day just wasn't going to work out?

R: No, I didn't even think about that. Thought about getting off of there and getting home safely. All I wanted to do was get home. And I believe that's the way most of us men felt at the time (Reagan).

Reagan's account gives the picture of an ordinary man caught up in extra-ordinary circumstances. He was too busy to be overcome by the fear that everyone felt. They had to concentrate on the task at hand: getting off of that beach and out of the line of fire. Half the men in the platoon had been lost in the initial landing. Reagan and the other survivors from his platoon made it to their objective after a long and grueling day.

How did Reagan's platoon of soldiers hold themselves together? Part of the answer is found in group training—the induction and indoctrination of the troops who made up the Army. Stouffer writes:

> The rigid and complexly hierarchical Army organization, with its accompanying set of formal rules, was the Army's main answer to the stress and confusion of battle. The soldier was not an individual atom in the tide of warfare; he was an integral part of a vast system of discipline and coordination. The chain of command was implemented by stringent sanctions for failures to conform. Men faced combat in tightly organized formal groups, and were held in those groups by the ultimate sanctions their society wielded, including the power, almost never used, of punishment by death. Thus, the individual in combat was simultaneously guided, supported, and coerced by a framework of organization (Stouffer et al.).

In other words, part of what propelled these men forward was the organizational pull of the group. The glue that made this pull effective was seen in the societal norms and expectations that pulled the soldier further and further into the unit, until he felt compelled to act as the others, and that to not do so, would become unthinkable. This was a combination of external and internal coercion. It had to be done quickly in order to turn an average citizen into a soldier who could perform missions under fire. One wounded veteran who served in the Sicily and Italian campaign described it this way in the Stouffer study, "You get a habit of taking orders when you're in training so that when they tell you to do something, you do so without thinking".

Fighting for the Team with Faith

Empirical data from the Stouffer study suggests that more often than not, soldiers performed better and did their mission because they felt a strong bond and loyalty to their unit. They could not let the team down. But faith and prayer also played a role alongside the team motivation in moving them forward and to maintain their composure. Daryl Whitfield made this remark about his faith at Normandy:

> The worst battle in Normandy for me was at a crossroads near a town. A guy from my unit captured some German artillerymen. I remember learning how to talk to God when a German 88 {Author's note: anti-tank} gun was firing at me at a place called Hill 131[21] (Whitfield).

In the same table, parallel comparisons are shown for the men who did and who did not say that it helped them a lot to think that they "couldn't let the other men down." This provides an interesting contrast, since the differences are for the most part small. They consistently indicate that (1) one was helped a lot by thinking that one cannot let the other men down was associated with lower fear and higher self-confidence and willingness for combat, whereas (2) saying that prayer helped a lot was associated with the opposite characteristics. When scores on a scale of psychoneurotic symptoms and rank are simultaneously controlled, it turns out that saying that prayer helped a lot, and saying that it helped a lot to think that one could not let the other men down,

---

[21] The German 88mm Anti-tank Gun was one of the most well know n weapons in World War II. It was used in many variations against both ground and air targets.

were thus related to the men's reported battle reactions in 19 out of the 20 sub-comparisons. The difference in pattern is consistent and remains when the influences of rank and personality differences are ruled out as much as possible.

Thus, according to Stouffer et al. (1949), some men who were more confident in the group had less need of prayer, and those who were less sure tended to pray more. Together the two factors played an important role in keeping soldiers in the fight. In terms of leadership traits, these are faith and fraternity, and they played a joint role:

- Faith in a higher power and faith in your team.
- Fraternity—comradeship with one's fellow soldiers as well as feeling the presence of someone else unseen who is watching over you.

When men were questioned on combat motivation, "when the going got tough," they provided several explanations on how they and their leaders handled the stress and found motivation. We have seen the attitudes towards leaders in Tables 2 and 3 in Chapter 13. In both cases, prayer was a motivating factor, but also, that it helped to think "that you couldn't let the other men down." Specifically, in the survey of men from the European theater, this was the primary motivating factor in keeping leaders going, 81% for responsibility to others versus 57% for prayer. For enlisted soldiers, the ratio was reversed, with 83% for prayer, but 56% for "couldn't let the other men down." Nevertheless, this was still double the percentage of the other factors of the questionnaire, such as "finish the job, hatred of the enemy," and "what we are fighting for". This statistic repeats itself in table after table of surveys of veterans regardless of education or rank. The main difference being that prayer (faith) was a lesser factor in the officer statistics. It should also be noted that perhaps at the time when the surveys were conducted, combat motivation might have been more of a blanket term for many aspects of internal mechanisms that kept soldiers focused on and able to endure combat. If this were the case, then a more appropriate way to describe the phenomenon is that prayer was a factor in sustaining combat motivation. The empirical data from Stouffer and the Army suggests that faith and fraternity were critical factors in getting soldiers through the rough times. While these are not the same as motivation, they were factors that made up a critical part of the total motivation template.

Taking care of one's men or a buddy was also the most referred to reason in the oral history analysis done of the D-Day 60 Veterans for leadership type actions and why they did what they did. However, Whitfield's example of learning to talk to God is illustrative of the faith factor in these men.

No other choice

Henry French was a Sergeant who, along with his soldiers, got separated from the main body of his company during the early inland fighting at Normandy. He was mentioned in another section as a first line leader. In this section, we look at Sergeant French from the point of view of analyzing why he and his men moved forward. We have already discussed several other factors. Is there another factor or reason, and does it relate to our discussion on emergent leadership at D-Day? The answer is, "yes." This trait may have several descriptive terms, but one that is fitting for a leader in this case is being resolute: when there is no other choice but to go on and do the best one can do with what one has. Sergeant French led 15 men and was awarded a Bronze Star Medal for helping out a machine gunner and was wounded in action twice. He describes the actions of his men and himself, and also shows other ways that he was a good leader by taking care of another group of soldiers who got mixed up with his in the chaos of the fight:

I: You just wanted to do your job and get home.

F: Just wanted to do my job and take care of my men.

I: What was your rank?

F: Sergeant.

F: Well, I just had, uh, you know, about fifteen men under me . . . I'm not bragging but I had no trouble . . . you take control out there.

I: The regular soldiers . . . .

I: They thought highly of you?

F: Well, yes, they did.

I: They wanted to go with you. They thought that you weren't going to do anything stupid.

F: No.

I: Well that's a good sign of a non-commissioned officer. You know, you don't get people unnecessarily hurt.

F: No. No.

I: So, you get to the top of the hill. You get reinforced up there? Or did they . . .

F: Just keep moving in. Coleville was our objective. But anyway, when we got to the top of the hill, I don't know how we got separated but myself and oh, I'd say fifteen to twenty more men, got separated from the Company Commander, and the Company and we just taken a dark trail, no road, and went around and . . . we were out there . . . so we got into the woods up there and we got a little sniper fire but it was getting too late than in that. So we just said well we'll find a place somewhere and we found a big ditch and we all got in it and . . . hunkered down for the night. And the next morning we got in touch with the Company telling 'em that, so (Inaudible) found their company and we found ours.

I: Oh so you had, you had like a mixed unit when you moved out . . . you might have had a couple of guys with the 29th with you and you were with the 1st and everybody was just moving.

F: It didn't matter. We were just trying to take care of each other.

I: You knew there was only one way to go, right?

F: Yeah. Only one way to go.

I: Yeah. At some point, did they sort things out and get everyone kind of all gathered in their proper units?

F: Uh-huh . . . we all got back to the unit . . . it was chaos (French).

SGT French really makes a key distinction in one segment of his account:

I: You just wanted to do your job and get home.

F: Just wanted to do my job and take care of my men (French).

Although we do not hear the tone he used, it does not matter. SGT French's focus was to do his job and take care of his men. This was a man who led his men through multiple periods of heavy fighting. As a leader, though, he was not looking for recognition. He simply did what had to be done. He had 15 men, and then another group almost as large that he eventually was shepherding through the skirmishes around them, leading them to shelter to "hunker down." Eventually, he was able to get back to his unit. He had no other option but to perform as a leader because not doing so would have most likely resulted in the deaths of not only him, but possibly the entire group. He kept his men going, and got the mission done.

Another trait that emerged from the combat experiences was a situational awareness that had to develop quickly or a soldier would not survive. 1LT Robert Landis gave his thoughts about the emergence of this survival trait:

I was waiting for hand to hand combat. We knew, you hear the German burp gun, the Schneizzer machine pistol. {Editor's Note: The Schnauser MP 40 Machinen Pistole was a nicknamed the "burp" gun because of its distinct sound.} You've never been in combat to hear those things coming closer to you, didn't take us long until everyone knew what a Schneizzer was. We didn't learn that. We never learned what the Germans had, or what a machine pistol is or what it sounded like until we got into battle. We'd been through an infiltration course in the States, so we knew what it was like to have bullets roaring over your head and staying close to the ground, but then you hear that Schneizzer, wow. It's getting closer and closer, and you think where are they going to come, you're aware of everything. All of your senses, you've got to be aware, we're in the dark. So they're on patrol and they're looking for us (Landis).

Summary

The compelling drive that brought the men ashore at the beaches of Normandy had many components. This chapter has identified several examples of these components in action. These include the following:

> ➤ Social Pressure—the need to perform one's duty because of the thought of how society and peers would react if one did not do their best to complete the mission.
> ➤ Fraternal loyalty—The bond that was developed by the members of the units that went ashore or jumped from the planes on D-Day. The men performed because they could count on each other to do their part of the mission. Their shared hardships and common experiences became this bond which held them together, no matter what the situation.
> ➤ Personal faith—The belief that a higher power played a role in helping them to go through the crisis an individual was facing, whether it was in terms of protecting the individual from harm, or to serve as a source of re-assurance during a crisis.
> ➤ Training—The regularity of giving and taking orders, following procedures and practice of repetitious actions that eventually became second nature to the soldier when ordered to move forward and perform his duty.

> ➤ Noble courage—The courage leaders, especially those on the ground and on point, displayed when responsible or when they felt responsibility for the welfare and lives of those around them and then took actions to lead them through the crisis situation, whether under fire or otherwise.
> ➤ Additionally, the emergence of the situational awareness survival traits should be noted in this summation, as a leader would have had to have these as a pre-requisite to have survived combat.

This chapter has explored many reasons why they did it and some of the traits that were required to survive in battle. The personal accounts of the veterans studied attest to the fact that there were many factors that played a role in this. However, we believe the six components identified above played prominent roles in getting the majority of soldiers to function and survive on the battlefield as team members and leaders. Likewise, the leadership traits that were brought out were catalyzed by one or more of these same factors. If this was leadership, and not simply courage, then there should be evidence that many of these men went beyond the initial germination of the leadership within them and went on to become successful leaders at higher levels and continued to grow. We shall discuss this in the next chapter as we take a look at what they did beyond D-Day.

CHAPTER 10

THE D-DAY EFFECT

Introduction

Having looked at many accounts of the veterans from D-Day, we now examine whether leadership at D-Day and the traits which surfaced were behaviors that were long term and lasting in nature. We have seen many examples where the soldiers stood up and emerged as leaders, through circumstance, training, and personal initiative.

Many people define epochs in their lives by large events or disasters. For many people of the current generation it might be the day President Kennedy was shot, the Challenger disaster, or the attacks on the World Trade Center. For the generation of veterans in this study, the attack on Pearl Harbor was an event that was burned into their memories.

But D-Day was different, it was a life-defining event. Several veterans described D-Day and the events during that time in Before and After terms; the campaign was the defining rite of passage for them.

Arnold Franco from the Ninth Air Force described his experience during this time in this excerpt from his account. He gave the following account about how the war changed him:

> . . . it definitely changed my life. The fact that we got to Paris when it was liberated; I became 21. I think Andy Rooney wrote a book called My War. He said anybody who had been to Paris at the time of liberation as a young man, that's the high point of his life. And, actually, it was. I mean, I felt my whole life afterwards was an anti-climax. I mean I got home, I started a business, I raised a family, I have four kids, I'm very active, still working. As you can see I am an active person. But, that was the high point in my life (Franco).

Joseph Bruckner Sullivan described D-Day and its effect on his life in this way:

> In hindsight of years gone by, it was sort of a watershed event in my life. At 79, I still think in terms of "before Normandy" and "after Normandy." The day I got married. But of course Normandy was a big event in a young life. Of course, I saw a lot of carnage of the war. I've been strong on national defense, so no one will ever be put through that terrible task again (Sullivan).

Will Tucker related what General Ridgway told him and his fellow paratroopers just prior to the invasion:

> I knew we were getting ready to do something big. I remember General Ridgeway speaking to us and how he said we "would be involved in the greatest event of our century, and some of you will make it and some of you will not make it back" (Tucker).

Whether historians agree on the magnitude of D-Day's actual impact on the course of the war or whether it was the battle of the century is up to the historians to continue to argue. But it is clear from the accounts of the men in this study that most of them would agree that it was an extraordinary, pivotal point in all of their lives. It changed them and stayed with them.

Ray Tolleson, the Ranger whose account was presented earlier, described the lifetime bond and resultant success enjoyed by his fellow Rangers and himself as a result of their experiences in these terms:

> . . . I don't know if you're aware of the Ranger Battalions of World War II . . . Well, we had formed in the States way before we had been training . . . we have a tremendous amount of men that have been so successful. You could tell the grade of Ranger we had because they have been so successful in life, and here we are . . . (Tolleson).

Both of these accounts reflect the general confidence and pride that many of these veterans felt. Arnold Franco described it as a crusade. They show the excitement they felt by being part of something truly important. Ray Tolleson's account is tempered by the sadness of seeing the passing of his comrades after so many years. He manages to include a dramatic and tragic history for his Ranger comrades in only a few sentences. He illustrates the *esprit de corps* that stayed with the unit, long after the war, as illustrated in his references to the wild, rowdy meetings in Chicago. He also speaks of the tremendous success that a large number of them went on to enjoy, which he attributes directly to what he terms "the grade" of Ranger. No further words are necessary to explain what he so clearly stated.

Ralph Widener brought up another lesson learned, although not from D-Day, but one he felt important to mention:

> I don't know. I grew up during the Depression years and I know how tough that was and everything. And my dad always said if you can, put away at least ten or twenty percent of whatever you make and I was able to do that always (Widener).

Widener's views on D-Day were reflective of the values of his time. He and many others from our account weathered D-Day and then went back home to rebuild their lives. They did this through hard work and using the lessons they learned about life, appreciating the things that perhaps others who had not experienced such events might take for granted, even today. The combination of the effects of war and the Depression went deep into him and many others from this study. The composite character of a D-Day survivor was one of a hard worker, able to endure unimaginable horror in battle, never knowing whether he would live to see the next day. This was a person who understood that there was a job to be done once the battle and the war were over. The knowledge of a termination, an eventual finality to their efforts gave them hope. The traits that emerged as part of their experiences gave many of them the tools to go on to lead very successful lives.

How does one define personal success? Captain Milnor Roberts, aide to the V Corps Commander, went on to become a major general. His account of loyalty and observations of leadership while working as the aide to the V Corps Commander has been discussed earlier. But he was only one of many men from the group who went on to achieve above average success.

The 82nd Airborne's Will Tucker went on to become a lawyer as well and summed up his greatest success as the fellowship of the men he served with:

> The whole war was a challenge. There was no particular moment for me when some battle in the war would stick out as a special challenge. It was all about discipline. You had to accept the fact that you could get killed. Once you did that, you knew what to do. I became a sergeant and was with the company the entire time. My single greatest success was the fellowship I have maintained my entire life with the men I served with.

> After World War II I finished law school. During the early 1960's I was a lawyer for the Kennedy administration in the Commerce Department. I was able to author books based on my war experience in the 82nd Airborne Division (Tucker).

Tucker identifies two solid and consistent traits seen throughout this study: his loyalty and bond with those who served with him, and the discipline which enabled him to get through his challenges. Discipline is a trait that made the difference between success and failure for many of the men in the group. It was noted in earlier accounts. It was what Ralph Widener was talking about when he was discussing saving money over the years. It was what made men like MG Roberts go back and find the family of a comrade killed on the beach at D-Day. It was a self-discipline that drove leaders to keep going then, and to keep going afterwards, and eventually to come back 60 years later to speak of their moments in history.

Harold McCauley went through D-Day, completed the European Campaign, and then headed home to Wisconsin. McCauley applied the principles of consistency, self-discipline and hard work in his civilian life and went on to become a success in the civilian world. He ended up running the family farm and raising a family of 10 successful children:

I went back to camp McCoy Wisconsin and got discharged. I had three different jobs in Madison Wisconsin, one was a Greyhound bus driver, and I could have gone to work in two weeks at Chevrolet as a parts man. I could pick the job on a Monday morning. I went home to get clothes and my dad got me to take over the farm. I raised 10 kids. They all went to college, and paid for the farm. Eight years after I bought it, I rented it for many years. My wife is a nurse, I have five daughters who are nurses and one a doctor. I have a granddaughter who is a doctor at St Mary's Hospital in Madison, Wisconsin (McCauley).

Artilleryman, Major Raymond Mason of 4th Armored Division, was successful after the war as well—both in business and in continued military service. The personal initiative and leadership he displayed while a young lieutenant leading soldiers carried over into his professional life. He also went into the family business, but he had to start over when he arrived back home. Later in his life, because of his expertise in trucking, he ended up becoming a major general in the Army and retired after a long career in the Reserves:

> I came out of the war and went back into the family business. My father had been a pioneer trucker, but he had gone out of business during the war.
>
> The Army started up the Army Reserve Schools. I had a good record and knew more about artillery than most people. So I figured I should become an instructor in the service school . . . One thing led to another and the next thing you know I was in the 83rd Infantry Division and eventually became the Division Artillery Commander.
>
> They wanted me in Washington for the Army Materiel Command because I knew how to drive a truck and shift gears with a diesel engine. They didn't have too many generals that knew that. From then on I got a two star job in the Pentagon, and finally retired.

Mason goes on to talk about how he was successful in business. He went into the cattle business and eventually owned three ranches in Florida, as well maintaining a trucking business in Columbus, now run by his son. Mason's account closes with a note on his humble beginnings, sharing a perspective that many soldiers of his generation share. He lived in an austere environment, saving a dollar here and there, all while undergoing the hardship and regimentation of military life:

> When I became a lieutenant in 1941 after ROTC we were paid $125 a month. That was not very much even then. After we got married I got a $40 housing allowance a month. She came to live with me in Watertown, NY in a little beat up half assed apartment. We lived on 160 dollars a month and saved some of it. I was on duty on post and not allowed to come in except on Wednesday night and on weekends. I had to be back for reveille on Monday morning (Mason).

Major General Raymond Mason was a successful leader. He had to work hard to become a success, but like others in the study, he used the skills and traits that emerged from his service at D-Day and beyond to make this possible.

Bob Cleary of the 83rd Recon Troop, 83rd Infantry Division was another veteran who went on to success. He came through Omaha Beach as part of Patton's Third Army. After the war he graduated from Ohio Wesleyan University, stayed in the Active National Guard, and retired as a colonel. As a young Lieutenant, he was on point in the 83rd Recon. Out front and away from the safety of the main body of troops, Cleary and his men had to be self-disciplined and display initiative and teamwork in order to survive. One important aspect of his service occurred some ten months after D-Day, when during a recon mission he and his men pulled up to one of Hitler's concentration camps. Such a profound event was only a part of what made up his individual road to leadership. Cleary describes his mission as part of the recon element:

> My claim to fame (chuckle), if you want to call it that, is that I'm the first American officer to liberate a German concentration camp . . . In Ohrdruf(dorf) . . . and that was a "sub-camp" of Buchenwald and it's the camp where

Eisenhower, Churchill, Bradley, Patton, Montgomery all came to within a week and Patton was so upset by what he saw, he went back in the town, got a hold of the mayor, and had him bring everybody in that town to the camp . . . walking . . . there were two guards on the gate. We shot one and the other ran off. Inside . . . we set up a perimeter defense. The guys in the barracks were so weak they could hardly get out of bed. But they had . . . ten (10) foot by forty (40) foot dugout holes you know and bodies were all in these holes. Then they had spread lye all over them to try to hurry their {decomposition} (inaudible) and uh, it was the worst sight I have ever experienced in my life. They were stacked eight (8) feet high like cordwood. Dead you know. Dead just inside there . . . and, one of my guys gave a candy bar to an inmate and within thirty seconds he threw it up. Couldn't handle it at all and we left. We called troop headquarters, got our instructions to wait there until 354th Infantry or one of the companies came and relieved us, and we went out on a new mission. So, I was not there for all of the hoopla . . . But, all of the people who came to Ohrdorf, the mayor and his wife and all, when they went back home after seeing it, the mayor and his wife committed suicide . . . Our mission was eyes and ears of the division. We were supposed to be out in front. We weren't supposed to engage unless we got in trouble . . . we were given assignments every couple of days in different sectors . . . that was the job of the recon troop. We ended up on the Czech border and lost a fair number of men. I managed a Silver Star and two Bronze Stars with oak leaf clusters, two purple hearts and a French Croix de Guerre (Cleary).

Later in the interview, Cleary comments about his feelings about the waste of lives and material in the War. His older brother was killed in action and was posthumously promoted to major. He avoids going too deeply into his own thoughts of the camp liberation, and it seems more out of respect for the lives lost and to avoid drawing attention to his own actions as a leader. Certainly with multiple awards of the Silver Star and the Purple Heart he had achieved many feats of leadership in action. The lessons of his earlier life served Cleary well. He was not only a successful leader. He was also a successful parent:

> C: I had a boy in Florida, I mean in Miami, Oxford . . . And what's the one in Springfield? . . . Anyway, had one there. One at the University of Pennsylvania, Georgetown, one at the University of California. Six kids. Six colleges and a few Masters (degrees). It was all part of the trip.

> I: So, any overall feelings about the war?

> C: I get—I really—you know, I've been here before and I'm always in awe when I visit either the American or the German cemeteries. It really gets me . . . Because of the vast quantities, you know, just the terrible waste of all these young guys including my brother who was killed at the Battle of the Bulge. He had the 87th Recon Troop . . . He was a captain . . . Two days after he died he was promoted to major and of course he was older (Cleary).

Men like Bob Cleary and others discussed in this chapter saw some of the worst atrocities of humanity. Instead of self-destructing, they emerged as leaders. Instead of seeing only the senselessness of war and losing hope, they appreciated what life had to offer and imparted that to their children, passing the values of hard work, self-discipline, and their leadership on to them. They went on to live the American dream. For many of them, this success may have been because they understood why they had been fighting. Seeing what they were fighting for gave them a sense of closure for the violence they endured and participated in as soldiers. Eugene Cook describes this process with his account:

> I always tell everybody: I was only eighteen, and I turned nineteen just before Bastogne. I always told everybody that you never really got a hell of a good feel of what you were fighting for until we took the concentration camp at Landsburg. After that we had all these displaced persons. It was just a final recognition of what the hell you were fighting for. Other than that it wasn't too nice (Cook).

Summary

The picture that emerges of the D-Day soldier 60 years after surviving the battle and the war is one of a successful, but often humble, diligent, focused and resilient character. A composite taken from these accounts of how this leader looks:

> ➤ Resilient: Despite having seen countless horrors from the war the majority of these men went on to success because they were able to bounce back from the challenges and difficulties they faced.
> ➤ Diligent: The men in the study had the ability to stick with a project to success. This showed up early as they went through training and formative leadership challenges in the War, and was followed up by their continued affiliation with successful long term endeavors, such as continued military service or founding businesses.
> ➤ Focused: The D-Day veteran came back from the war with a sense of understanding of the world that others who had not experienced combat and the human tragedy to such a degree as they did, could not understand. They were able to see what the fighting was about and knew why they had been fighting in Europe. This left them with a more resolute view of what needed to be done, especially in terms of national defense issues, and explains why they continued their service, or answered the call once again in subsequent conflicts.
> ➤ Confident: The men who came back from the war were confident in themselves and their capabilities. Whether it was through the strong bond of fellowship developed in units like the Rangers, or an internal confidence that came from leading soldiers as a squad leader or platoon leader, the men who survived were transformed and empowered.

Additionally, these soldiers translated these traits into an example for their children to emulate, in both service and education. As many of the veterans recall, there was life before and after D-Day. The event had a profound impact on them, and what they experienced in Normandy was internalized and built into their permanent character. The circumstances of the war gave them no other option but to grow into their leadership roles or face elimination in the harsh circumstances of combat. The price for failure to lead was much higher than in the business world that they faced when they returned from the war. Having faced life or death based on a split second decision, they could better lead subordinates, keep challenges in perspective and complete tasks, as well as unleash a creativity that enabled so much of the American expansion in the years following the War.

CHAPTER 11

DISCUSSION OF
THEORETICAL FINDINGS

Introduction

THIS CHAPTER PRESENTS THE FINDINGS of our study when applied
to the hypothesis put forth in the beginning of this work: there is a core
of leadership competencies that emerge when people are put into crisis
situations regardless of their background. There are two models that are
presented here to illustrate how this theory functions. Additionally there
are several examples taken from earlier sections to show the practicality
of the model and how it works. It is by no means the only way to explain
leadership or why some people lead and others do not. But it does offer a
clear and concise explanation for those who carry the requisite leadership
material, maturity, and who by chance or design, happen to meet with
a triggering event that can cause the phenomena of leadership growth
catalyzed by the event.

We note two types of model: ELDC and ELOT, both defined in the
following section. One does not necessarily rule out or negate the effects
of the other. The principal difference is the time frame involved.

Discussion of findings in relation to Emergent Leadership During Crisis Hypothesis

Emergent Leadership During Crisis—ELDC

The accounts in the study evoked multiple examples of emergent
leadership during crisis, the descriptive term we use to describe the
process that occurs within individuals as crisis precipitates reaction, based
on circumstances of the event, the individual's readiness in terms of trait
maturity (the level of development of particular traits needed to act in
the situation), and the event itself.

Emergent Leadership Over Time—ELOT

The accounts showed that leadership also emerged over time. Many examples illustrated how training and development of the soldier prior to D-Day was a method of bringing out leadership traits and skills. This also catalyzed development from one level to another, as in CPT Goranson who went from enlisted soldier to company commander.

The qualifying factors for ELDC or ELOT are the circumstances, that is, the subject's trait maturity level, or readiness to act, the experience level, and the position (formal or informal). These factors come together and combine to produce the action that occurs when a precipitating event occurs. This could be a chance or planned event.

Our observations show that emergent leadership is catalyzed in similar fashion, but when events dictate, this development is expedited. The basic format that applies to either is:

Subject + Circumstance (Trait Maturity + Experience + Position) + Event = Leadership Action

The significant difference between ELDC and ELOT is the time involved. The following examples illustrate how this theory fits into the situations discussed at D-Day.

Case 1 shows an example of ELOT.

Case 1—Goranson p. 141

Subject + Circumstance (Trait Maturity + Experience + Position) + Event = Leadership Action

Goranson + (TM + D&C experience + Reg CDR-ROTC) + OCS Board = Commission

Ralph Goranson had a high work ethic and quickly assimilated into the Army. He entered the Army with some drill and ceremony experience from high school, where he was the regimental commander. This helped set him apart from his peers. He was given advanced levels of responsibility and sent to the OCS board where he passed, and then went on to OCS where received his commission.

Goranson + (TM + Add'l experience + PLT LDR) + Offer of CMD= CDR @ D-Day

As Goranson's level of leadership confidence was increased and his traits honed to a higher level of performance, he was noticed by his battalion commander, who offered him a company to command. He did not hesitate to accept it. He went on to lead his troops as a company commander at D-Day.

In Case 1, we see how Goranson developed as a leader in high school and went into the military with some level of leadership already apparent. His leadership emerged over time. After Officer Candidate School, he had to decide on the spot whether to take the command or not. Forced to act, he made his choice, and the resulting action allowed his leadership to continue to develop. If he had not taken the command, then his leadership development would have been delayed. He might never have had the same circumstances again for emergence of leadership to occur. However, because he was ready, and due to the increased pressure and need to perform under greater stress, Goranson's skills as a leader further developed. He ended up becoming one of a handful of Ranger company commanders at Normandy.

Case 2 is drawn from the earlier excerpt of SSG Paul Merriman's account of an accident that occurred during combat. This illustrates how ELDC is catalyzed by an event that forced Merriman to act. His prior experience and maturity level enabled him to act swiftly and decisively. At the same time, he was suddenly forced into a leadership position. This triggered the response in him that resulted in several lives being saved.

Case 2—Merriman

Subject + Circumstance (Trait Maturity + Experience + Position) + Event = Leadership Action

Merriman + Driver in a Convoy + Explosion= Took charge in aiding wounded

SSG Merriman was a driver in a convoy when a landmine was struck. He took charge in aiding the wounded and stayed with them and then went on to catch up to his unit.

Merriman's quote from the first chapter offers explanation why this rapid process occurred. One had to grow up in a hurry. There was no time for mistakes. If mistakes were made people died. Experiential learning was rapid. Young, inexperienced soldiers became veterans overnight. If not, they did not make it. Leadership had to emerge, because someone had to lead the way. As SSG Merrriman said, "It was always a sergeant or a corporal who would go out on point because somebody had to be in charge, the guy with the stripes (Merriman, p. 173)".

Multiple examples of ELDC occurred in soldiers throughout the D-Day beaches landing area, as well as among the paratroopers as they landed scattered across the hedgerows and fields. The two examples provided earlier from Norman Schein describe what process had to occur in order to survive on the battlefield. Schein took a direct leadership role when he was the leader of a two man team that went out on a decoy reconnaissance mission. Even though it was just the two men, Schein felt the leadership responsibilities of any leader. He had to perform his mission and get his team back to safety. When faced with the challenge of being caught behind enemy lines or going between vehicles in a

German convoy, Schein made the decision and took action. He knew the risks, weighed them and then did what was required. Later on, he saved his comrade's life during another mission. This shows that given the right circumstances this effect will occur again. Schein took risks at times, but as a leader he felt compelled to do so. He understood what would happen if he did not act, and so, even knowing there was danger, he did so without hesitation. His comment to his battle buddy, "yeah, but we made it" (Schein, p. 225) shows a level of relief, and also self-confidence. Schein appears to have matter-of-factly accepted the situation and acted the way he did as if it were second nature to him.

Schein was not supposed to succeed. Yet, he did. In the theoretical context of ELDC, we see how he carried the balance of traits, maturity, knowledge, and his position as leader of the two man team going on a reconnaissance as his circumstances. We see the catalyzing event being the mission and the dangers he successfully faced.

Case 3—Schein

Subject + Circumstance (Trait Maturity + Experience + Position) + Event = Leadership Action

Schein + (Trait Maturity + Experience + 1st line leader) + Encounter with Enemy = Successfully brought his buddy team through enemy lines.

Norman Schein was on a recon mission into enemy territory. He found a way to survive and got back to Allied HQ.

Schein's natural traits had been developed to some extent before the event. This was the maturation process. However, when placed in the leadership position and faced with the odds against him, Schein took action. This action required more than simply raw courage, it required quick thinking, the ability to calculate many different courses of action and to pick one. In another example, Schein saved his friend's life during a reconnaissance mission when they were hit by shrapnel from an artillery shell. He acted quickly to fight off the attack and then applied first aid to his friend and got him to medical safety as quickly as possible. He did not freeze up or simply wait for someone to come along and give him an order. Schein remarked on the reaction of the doctor, and the feedback he received for his actions. "The doctor came up to me and he said are you responsible for this?" I said "Yes sir." He gave me a hug and he said. "You just saved a man's life." If you hadn't gotten him here right away, he would have died (Schein, p. 226)." Thus, his leadership experience was also shaped by the additional positive reinforcement given for taking immediate action.

This shows how he was building on his leadership experience from the earlier recon mission where he evaded capture. Schein found himself in an even more challenging situation. Having already had a level of leadership developed over time (ELOT), plus recent experience, Schein was forced to go to an even more sophisticated level of leadership and action. It was no longer thinking of a way through a situation; he had to take immediate direct, life-saving measures, followed up by a complex series of events. His previous experience played a role in setting the groundwork, but he was ready to act because he carried the necessary innate skills or traits to succeed.

Case 4—Schein

Subject + Circumstance (Trait Maturity + Experience + Position) + Event = Leadership Action

Schein + (Trait Maturity + Experience + 1st line leader) + Encounter with Enemy/wounded comrade = Returns fire/ applies medical aid/ successfully bringing him to safety.

Norman Schein's jeep was hit and his buddy was seriously wounded. He returned fire, performed first aid, and proceeded back to Allied medical support.

Doc Scanlon showed three examples of ELDC in Chapter 1, citing circumstance meeting events and the action that he took. As the war progressed, he continued to be empowered and grew as both a leader, and, at times, a rebel. In Cases 5, 6, and 7, taken from accounts reviewed in Chapter 1, we see Scanlon's actions in the context of ELDC. In Case 5 he took immediate action to stop incoming fire and save the lives of the men around him by standing up to a lieutenant who was calling in fire to the wrong location. In Case 6 he used German prisoners for moving the wounded and was going to have them fed. When told by another lieutenant that they do not feed the enemy, Scanlon exemplified transformational leadership when he went ahead and took care of them and he again stood his ground and took care of the prisoners. Although it was a form of rebellion, it was also leadership because he recognized that the prisoners were his responsibility. Lastly, in Case 7, Scanlon stood up to a colonel who he was having a disagreement with over moving prisoners. His sense of mission overtook his training as a subordinate, allowing him to put the welfare of his patients first, regardless of what the consequences might mean.

Case 5—Scanlon

Subject + Circumstance (Trait Maturity + Experience + Position) + Event = Action

Scanlon + (Trait Maturity + Experience + 1st line leader) + confrontation with artillery officer =

Scanlon takes action to stop fire, confronts lieutenant, receives support from Major O'Malley after he explains situation.

Scanlon went on to receive the Bronze Star Medal for his actions. The situations were critical. Wounded were coming in and he didn't have enough soldiers to support him with the mission of carrying them around the aid station. The circumstances of all three situations put him at odds with officers who were senior to him. However, his personal traits as a leader emerged and he stood his ground. His actions enabled him to complete his mission and save lives.

> **Case 6—Scanlon**
>
> Subject + Circumstance (Trait Maturity + Experience + Position) + Event = Leadership Action
>
> Scanlon + (Trait Maturity + Experience + 1st line leader) + lieutenant refuses to allow over food for POWs. =
>
> Scanlon confronts the lieutenant and feeds his prisoners.

Scanlon's behavior was reinforced by the success of his earlier encounters with seniors when faced with mission challenges. Later in the war he had an altercation with a colonel and faced the possibility of court martial for disrespecting an officer. Case 7 shows this encounter:

> **Example 7—Scanlon**
>
> Subject + Circumstance (Trait Maturity + Experience + Position) + Event = Leadership Action
>
> Scanlon + (Trait Maturity + Experience + 1st line leader) + confronted by COL who impedes his mission of caring for the wounded.
>
> Cusses out Colonel and takes his jeep.

Scanlon may have gone too far in this example, but by this time he had seen plenty of fighting, and probably did not care about the consequences of his words or actions; he had a mission to do, and it could not wait. Scanlon's examples show that if given follow-on events, that leadership continues to grow and rise to the challenges an individual faces. It also illustrates that if this leadership grows unchecked or un-impacted by other styles, that the leader's own personality is reflected in the style of leadership. If his leadership opportunities had come in different ways, then he might not have emerged as a leader. His set of traits and behavior were suited to the circumstances around him and thus was able to successfully emerge as a leader, and more importantly to accomplish his task of saving lives on the battlefield.

Summary of Emergent Leadership Theory Observations

The preceding examples are only a small sampling of how multiple opportunities for leadership emerged during the course of the campaign at D-Day for the study group under the ELDC and ELOT model. Though there are plenty of other models that could be applied as well, this is a clear, efficient way to describe the process that occurs as a person's leadership emerges. Multiple circumstances demonstrated how this can be applied.

Additionally, it allows for an explanation on how one's leadership growth occurs: event and catalyst leads to further development and resets the base circumstance for the individual, allowing for a further phase of leadership development. This will occur until the individual plateaus, either because no further development is required, that is the level of development they have achieved is sufficient for their circumstances, or if the development is arrested by outside factors that detract or hinder the individual from further growth. These could be due to personality, professional issues, or any other of a number of reasons.

It is noteworthy that many of these same men continued in their development and went on to become civilian and military leaders at much higher levels. We reviewed several examples of this in the D-Day Effect chapter. It may be that the intensity of the catalytic event provides for a stronger long term leadership development phase. This could be explored by further study.

Emergent leadership during crisis (ELDC) and emergent leadership over time (ELOT) are two ways of defining a similar model and approach to the study of leadership development. The examples presented through the D-Day 60 accounts support this argument.

Leadership growth: ELOT and ELDC

Emergent leadership over time (ELOT) and emergent leadership during crisis (ELDC) differ significantly in how the process occurs in an individual. *ELOT is a gradual process and can be formal or informal. Growth and maturity in leadership can be attained through graduated levels of responsibility or progression through rank or educational milestones. On the other hand, ELDC occurs in bursts, is not a planned or phased development, and often occurs in unexpected ways.*

The study of the D-Day 60 Veterans gave us several examples of both ELDC and ELOT. The graphic model representation of the difference between the two can be illustrated by either a straight line or a curve, depending on the individual. If there are no major crises, it is possible that an individual progresses in a normally linear fashion, so long as he or she is able to pass the next milestone, measure, or rank. However, in the case of ELDC, this progression would be exponential, depending heavily on the circumstances, leadership maturity, and the event itself.

It is also possible for both ELDC and ELOT to be occurring at the same time. Thus, leadership growth can be attained and reinforced by formal schooling or developmental process, as well as key events that trigger leadership trait emergence and development. Goranson's account illustrates the growth he experienced as compared to other examples of soldiers who did not progress as far in rank and responsibility. The difference between the two is clear. But it is only one indicator of the kind of growth that occurred for Goranson versus others who might not have had the opportunities and circumstances for their leadership qualities to surface. A squad leader was responsible for 10 men, but a company commander was responsible for over one hundred. These values are only hypothetical, but the point is that key events along the way propelled Goranson ahead of his peers. Goranson carried the traits, but it took circumstances and events to bring them out. If Goranson had not had early training, or a command climate that recognized his talents or was willing to allow him to develop, where would he have ended up after four years? Furthermore, Goranson was not an anomaly. There were thousands of men who went from the enlisted ranks to the officer ranks during WWII (Stouffer et al, 1949). They were forced into leadership positions by the circumstances around them, and when the events called for it, had to perform in order for both themselves and their men to survive.

Summary of Emergent Leadership Theory Observations

The preceding examples are only a small sampling of how multiple opportunities for leadership emerged during the course of the campaign at D-Day for the study group under the ELDC and ELOT model. Though there are plenty of other models that could be applied as well, this is a clear efficient way to describe the process that occurs as a person's leadership emerges. Multiple circumstances demonstrated how this can be applied. Additionally, it allows for an explanation on how one's leadership growth occurs: event and catalyst leads to further development and resets the base circumstance for the individual, allowing for a further phase of leadership development. This would occur until the individual plateaus, either because no further development is required—that is, the level of development they have achieved is sufficient for their circumstances—or if the development is arrested by outside factors that detract or hinder the individual from further growth. These could be due to personality, professional issues, or any other of a number of reasons.

It is noteworthy that many of these same men continued in their development and went on to become civilian and military leaders at much higher levels. We reviewed several examples of this in the D-Day effect chapter. It may be that the intensity of the catalytic event provides for a stronger long term leadership development phase. This could be explored by further study.

Emergent leadership during crisis (ELDC) and emergent leadership over time (ELOT) are two ways of defining a similar model and approach to the study of leadership development. The examples presented through the D-Day 60 accounts give a good basis to the reasonableness of this argument.

CHAPTER 12

PERSONAL REFLECTIONS ON ELDC

CHAPTER II CONCLUDED WITH THE stark difference between ELDC and ELOT. Regardless of the circumstance, there is a place for the study of emergent leadership. The evidence of this has been presented, examined, and broken down into these two categories in our study. The comparison and contrast of the findings drives home the real lessons for today's leaders:

> -Individuals must be placed in real leadership positions of both accountability and responsibility in order to grow as leaders. They must be empowered to act, as well as to fail and regroup in order to maximize their growth development. This means more empowerment of individuals, making them commanders and chiefs instead of staff officers or managers.

> -Senior leaders have a responsibility to groom all subordinate leaders for promotion, regardless of personal feelings or subjective criteria. This is especially true in organizations like the military where an individual is very likely to get promoted to the next rank, especially if he or she has completed all basic job and professional development requirements.

Just as Goranson's performance improved with his increased responsibilities and rank, so is it likely this will occur with others in similar situations. Not everyone is a Goranson; but if an individual is going to get promoted, and it is commonplace for this to occur, then senior leaders are helping themselves and the organization by developing the skills of these subordinates with meaningful mentorship. Failing to do this and at the same time allowing personnel to be promoted without the requisite developmental positions only creates issues for future senior leaders who have to deal with a senior staff composed of personnel who may be just as smart or competent as anyone else, but do not have the background and experience required to be successful, or to successfully add their own talents to the organization.

> -Junior leaders and individuals can change the paradigm and overcome challenges by seeking out additional responsibilities, schooling, or other professional development. Their personal successes should not be defined by their rank or position but by what they are capable of accomplishing and how successful they have been as leaders at their level.

Not every person is going to become a general, or president of a company. However, if individuals look for and participate or act in ways to change the equation and overcome challenges, either real or simulated, then growth will occur—both personal and professional.

Fixing Average

If senior leaders are hesitant to place subordinates in positions where more responsibility and growth occurs because they do not have the confidence in them, then they must look at training opportunities to allow for growth. These training opportunities should differ from training events relating simply to work or the mission at hand. This will benefit the organization, individual, and ultimately the leader, who will get more productivity and performance from a previously untried performer, or an improved one who has passed critical milestones that reflect his or her potential to perform. There are many leadership training opportunities in the Army, but how many of them re-create the D-Day effect? Ranger School is one example of a course that spurs personal growth, but that is the exception and not the rule. The challenge that organizations face is to create these leadership settings to develop their leaders that will propel them and the organization to success.

Further Study

The study of emergent leadership during crisis has shown that this phenomenon exists and should be studied further. Studies on inter-generational leadership among families, where the phenomena can be compared with the actions of those raised prior to one war period versus those raised in another, would help highlight which of these traits are the most prevalent and constant. Studies involving subjects from previous conflicts would also show other aspects of emergent leadership which may manifest differently over time. That is, the same trait may be present or constant, but it may emerge under different circumstances. Soldiers of earlier wars, such as the American Civil War, Spanish American War, World War I, and World War II could be compared to soldiers of the Korean War, Vietnam, the Gulf War, and today's conflicts in Afghanistan and Iraq. Indeed, ELDC may appear differently from one theater to the next because of the types of challenges being faced. Another aspect of this is to look at ELDC in conventional war versus counter-insurgency conflicts. For example, in both Iraq and Afghanistan, the initial conventional combat experiences faced by soldiers were more typical of past conflicts. However, the nature of the two conflicts changed, and both became conflicts where most soldiers were dealing with an asymmetrical enemy who could come out of any place at any time. For soldiers deployed to Iraq and Afghanistan, the leadership challenges have been different in some ways but have also been strikingly similar in others. It is important to study this.

Furthermore, ELDC in World War II may have been encouraged and fostered better than in today's environment. America's Army in World War II was not a professional army. This contrasts with today's smaller, but more professionally-oriented one that has its own cultural mores that may or may not be consistent with those of the rest of American society. In many ways, the military might be in the lead on some issues, such as integration. Are the techniques developed for the World War II Army still present or appropriate to developing situations where ELDC can occur? In other words, if we take civilians from a technologically, freer-thinking society, and we put them into an Army requiring higher levels of mental agility and training than in the past, are we training them in a way that will maximize their performance and growth potential?

Other areas where the study of ELDC is important are found in countless civilian organizations. The television show, *The Office*, examines relationships in the office environment and shows different aspects of the hierarchical struggles in one corner of the business world. Leaders and managers in the business world can benefit from studying ELDC by creating and reinforcing a framework where subordinates can grow and fail, and then pick themselves back up. Is this utopian thinking? For short-term thinkers and people who are too focused on immediate results, it is. However, for business leaders who can see beyond this, the answer is no.

This demonstrates the importance of the earlier points on ways to foster better leadership through developing programs that will help ensure emergent leadership processes can occur. Boot camp experiences similar to those used to indoctrinate soldiers in the military have been a method used as a way to get teenagers with delinquency issues to straighten out. However, long-term, leadership development is not about yelling, marching, and boring, repetitive tasks. It is about developing the intrinsic motivation processes within a person to propel themselves forward. The study of ELDC shows that the way to trigger the response necessary to grow as a leader, (and coincidentally as a by-product, to become a better citizen), is to have programs in place to make people responsible to work with others and lead in challenging conditions.

The question of whether these challenging conditions can be replicated for people without being caught in a firefight or going to Ranger school is "yes." Goranson and many of his peers were not under fire until well after they were on their way to become leaders or were already leaders in their own right because of critical situations where they had to act. Nearly all people have had moments in their lives when they felt their backs were up against a wall and they had to perform well or make a critical decision. Such moments create the conditions where ELDC occurs. There are many ways where ELDC is replicated in everyday life. Countless sports programs foster good leadership values. Student government projects and work place initiatives such as self-directed working teams are all ways that leadership can be developed.

The challenge for mentors and current leaders is to create more opportunities for this to happen. For example, sports programs that encourage only a select few to be leaders on the field might be better changed so that everyone on the team has a constant stake and role in the outcome.

One colleague of mine used the analogy of football versus rugby. In football, he said, everyone on the team is important, but clearly the quarterback, wide receivers, and other star positions have a more prominent role. These roles do not shift. On the other hand, in rugby, it is an asymmetrically competitive environment. Team members must work with every other member on the field to pass and carry the ball down the field. It is truly a team effort for the entire 80 minutes of the match.

My account is no story of battle leadership in crisis. I had a few challenges while deployed to Iraq, but nothing I could ever compare with those of the WWII 60 Veterans whose interviews are reported in this study. Nevertheless, the parallels of those experiences can be found in my own life experiences, and they have shaped me. I made choices along the way that enabled me to develop into an effective leader.

The key to exploiting the experiences of ELDC and applying it in an organization is to apply a consistent, steady, positive leadership style and to create an environment that allows for growth. The medium for developing leaders can be as varied as the challenges that befall people. The real key is empowerment, working within an atmosphere where one has opportunities to lead, develop, and yes, to fail. Only then will the person really be intrinsically motivated and own his or her mission. From this, individuals will gain the energy and spirit needed to become effective leaders.

I consider myself to be a product of ELDC because of those moments where I had to act and take charge in the many tests I had along the way and the combination of circumstances and events I faced along the way forced the traits within me to develop and emerge.

People recognized that although young and untrained, I had potential to develop into a leader. They provided me the leadership opportunities to grow. They helped put me into positions where I would develop as a leader, even though I did not know it at the time. The personal challenge for me has been to continue that chain and help others to achieve whatever their highest potential for leadership may be.

Leaders cannot develop alone in a vacuum—it requires circumstances and events to trigger their growth.

Emergent leadership tomorrow

The study of emergent leadership during crisis has taken us full circle back to the ideals of the ancient Greek school where young leaders were developed by great scholars who mentored them. If there is any final word on this subject, it is that service seems to be the constant that brings out the best in every leader. Effective organizational leadership requires this as a pre-requisite, and it is sorely needed in today's challenging business climate. Those who are willing to serve more, and understand what it means to be a servant to those whom they lead, may profit more in the long-run than their peers.

The veterans in our study took care of their troops and saw to their needs and the needs of the mission. They understood they had a higher calling. They epitomized selfless service, and their service saved lives and influenced the world in many positive ways. As further studies are done in ELDC and other aspects of leadership during crisis, this point should be kept in mind. Wars may change from generation to generation. Business environments may change and go from boom to bust economies. Sports teams may have dynasties and then become perennial losers. But over time, in all of these situations, the constant process of developing leaders is ongoing, preparing the world for the next generation of leaders regardless of success or failure. Thus, one should have confidence in the future, knowing that in a thousand different ways, parallel leadership experiences are occurring. We can be sure that when called, the next greatest generation will be there to pick up where the previous one left off, ready to carry the torch of leadership into the future.

REFERENCES

Ambrose, S. (1985). *Pegasus Bridge: June 6, 1944*. New York: Simon & Schuster.

Ambrose, S. (1992). *Band of brothers*. New York: Simon & Schuster

Ambrose, S. (1997). *Citizen soldiers*. New York: Simon & Schuster.

Astor, G. (1994). *June 6, 1944: The voices of D-Day*. New York: Dell Publishing.

Bass, B. (1990). From transactional to transformational leadership: Learning to share the vision. *Organizational Dynamics*, (Winter) pp 19-31.

Belasco, J. & Stayer, R. (1993). *Flight of the buffalo: Soaring to excellence, learning to let employees lead*. New York: Warner Books.

Bennis, W. & Nanus, B. (1997). *Leaders: Strategies for taking charge*. New York: Harper Collins.

Berg, B.L. (2007) *Qualitative research methods for the social science*, London: Pearson.

Blake, R.R, & Mouton, J. (1964). *The managerial grid*. Houston, TX: Gulf.

Blanchard, K. (1969) Comments on "College Boards of Trustees: A need for Directive Leadership." *The Academy of Management Journal*, Vol. 12, No. 1 (Mar., 1969), pp.124-126.

Blanchard, K., Zigarmi, D. & Nelson, R.B. (1993). Situational leadership after 25 years: A retrospective. *Journal of Leadership Studies*, 1(1),22-36.

Blanchard, K., Zigarmi, P. & Zigarmi, D (1985). *Leadership and the one minute manager*. Escondido, CA: Blanchard Training and Development.

Boje, D., The leadership box (revised 2003), retrieved 27 January 2007 from (http://cbae.nmsu.edu/~dboje/teaching/338/traits.htm)

Brinkley, D. (2005). *The boys of Pointe du Hoc: Ronald Reagan, D-Day, and the U.S. Army 2nd Ranger Battalion*. New York: Harper Perennial.

Brokaw, T. (2001). *The greatest generation*. New York: Dell Publishing.

Cawthon, D. (2002). *Philosophical foundations of leadership*. New Brunswick, NJ: Transaction Publishers.

Covey, S. (1990). *The seven habits of highly effective people.* Philadelphia: Franklin—Covey.

Crane, S. (1895). *The red badge of courage,* retrieved 25 January 2006 from (http://en.wikipedia.org/wiki/The_Red_Badge_of_Courage)

Doyle, M. & Smith M. (2008). Classical leadership. Retrieved 2 February 2008 from (http://www.infed.org/leadership/traditional_leadership.htm)

Dienesch, R. Liden, R. (1986). Leader-Member Exchange Model of leadership: A critique and further development. *The Academy of Management Review,* Vol. 11, No. 3 (Jul., 1986), pp. 618-634.

Dunegan, K., Uhl-Bien, M., & Duchon, D. (2002). LMX and subordinate performance: The moderating effects of task characteristics. *Journal of Business and Psychology,* Vol. 17, No. 2 (Dec., 2002), pp. 275-285.

Fiedler, F.E. (1967). *A contingency model of leadership effectiveness.* New York: McGraw Hill.

Fleishman, E.A., Mumford, M.D., Zacarro, S. J., Levin, K.Y. & Korotkin, A. L. (1991). Taxonomic efforts in the description of leader behavior: A synthesis and functional interpretation. *Leadership Quarterly,* 2(4), pp. 245-287, JAI Press Inc.

Franco, A.C. (1998). *Code to victory: Coming of age in World War II by Arnold C. Franco, as told to Paula Aselin Spellman.* Manhattan, KS: Sunflower University Press.

Fussell, P. (1989). *Wartime: Understanding and behavior in the Second World War.* Oxford: Oxford University Press.

Gabert, T.E., (2006). *Leadership Perspective: Class Notes.* University of Oklahoma, Summer, 2006.

Gardner, J. (1989). *On leadership.* New York City: Free Press, retrieved 25 January 2007 from Doyle, Michele Erina and Smith, Mark K, Classical Leadership http://www.infed.org/leadership/traditional_leadership.htm

Goleman, D. (1995). *Emotional intelligence—why it can matter more than IQ.* New York: Bantam Books.

Graef, C. (1983) *The Situational Leadership Theory: A critical view*[1]. The Academy of Management Review, Vol. 8, No. 2 (Apr., 1983), pp. 285-291.

Graen, G. & Uhl-Bien, M. (1995). Relationship-based approach to leadership: Development of leader member exchange (LMX) theory of leadership over 25 years: Applying a multi-level multi-domain perspective. *Leadership Quarterly*, 6(2), pp. 219-247. JAI Press Inc.

Groves, B. (2006). MG Matthew Ridgway as the 82d Airborne Division Commander: A case study on the impact of vision and character in leadership. *The Land Warfare Papers*, No. 59, Oct. 2006.

Hastings, M. (1984). *Overlord: D-Day and the Battle of Normandy*. New York: Vintage Books.

Hanselman, D. (2005). Reserve soldiers capture history supporting 60th Anniversary of D-Day, *Army Reserve Magazine*, Winter, 2005.

Hersey, P., Blanchard, K., & Johnson, D. (2001). *Management of organizational behavior: Leading human relations* (8th Edition). Upper Saddle River, NJ: Prentice-Hall.

House, R. & Hogan, J. (2002). Leadership and socio-political intelligence. In Riggio, R., Murphy, S. & Pirozzolo (Eds.), *Multiple intelligences and leadership* (pp75-88). San Francisco: Jossey-Bass.

House, R. & Howell, J. (1992). Personality and charismatic leadership. *LeadershipQuarterly*, (3)2, 81-108

House, R. & Additya, R. (1997). The social scientific study of leadership: Quo vadis? *Journal of Management, 23*, 409-473.

Katz, R. (1955). Skills of an effective administrator. *Harvard Business Review*, Jan-Feb 1955, pp. 33-42.

Klann, G. (2007). *Building character: Strengthening the heart of good leadership*. San Francisco: Jossey-Bass

Kouzes, J., & Posner, B. (2003). *The leadership challenge*. San Francisco: Jossey-Bass.

Landsberger, Henry A. (1958). *Hawthorne revisited: Management and the worker, its critics, and developments in human relations in industry*. Cornell University, Ithaca, New York.

Locke, E.A., Kirkpatrick, S. & Associates. (1991). *The essence of leadership: The four keys to leading successfully*. New York: Lexington Books.

Lord, R., DeVader, C., & Alliger, G. (1986). Leadership: Do traits matter? *The Executive*, 5, 48-60.

Lowe, J. (1998). *Jack Welch speaks: Wisdom from the world's greatest business leader*. New York: John Wiley & Sons.

Lowe, J. (1998). *Bill Gates speaks: Insight from the world's greatest entrepreneur*. New York: Wiley & Sons.

Magee, B (2001). *The story of philosophy*. Singapore: Dorling Kindersley.

McClelland, D. (1985). See House, 1997.

Mumford, D. J., Zaccaro, S.J., Harding, F.D., Jacobs, T.O. & Fleishman, E.A. (2000). Leadership skills for a changing world: Solving complex social problems. *Leadership Quarterly*, 11(1), 23, 2000.

Natemeyer, W., & McMahon, T. (2001). *Classics of organizational behavior*. Long Grove, IL: Waveland Press.

Northouse, P. (2004). *Leadership: Theory and practice* (3rd Edition). Thousand Oaks, CA: Sage Publications.

Peters T. & Austin, N. (1985). *A passion for excellence: The leadership difference*. New York: Random House

Peters, T. & Waterman, R. (1982). *In search of excellence: Lessons from America's best run companies*. New York: Grand Central Publishing.

Phillips, D. (1992). *Lincoln on leadership: executive strategies for tough times*. New York: Warner Books

Pierce, M. (2002). Personal Notes: Vampire O/C Team staff ride to Normandy. Unpublished.

Pierce, M. (2003). Personal Notes: Vampire O/C Team staff ride to Monte Cassino. Unpublished.

Reddin, W.J. (1967, April) The 3D management style theory. *Training and Development Journal,* 8-17.

Robbins, S. (2005). *Essentials of organizational behavior*. Upper Saddle River, NJ: Pearson Prentice Hall.

Rodgers, J. (2006). Unpublished Statistics course notes. University of Oklahoma, taken in Mannheim, Germany, Spring 2006.

Ross and Offerman (1990). See House, 1992.

Roth-Douquet, K. and Shaeffer, F. (2001). *AWOL: The unexcused absence of America's upper classes from military service*. London: Harper-Collins.

Rusaw, A. (2001). *Leading public organizations: An interactive approach*. Fort Worth: Harcourt College Publishers.

Rush, R., 31 August 2007, Assistant Director, Center for Military History, notes from email discussion on military leadership.

Sadler, P. (1997). *Leadership*. London: Kogan.

Schofield, Major General John M. (1879) Excerpt from address to the Corps of Cadets, 11 August 1879. West Point, NY

Seiler, W., Baudheim, E., & Shuelke, L. (1982). *Communication in business and professional organizations*. Reading, MA: Addison-Wesley Publishing.

Shadley, R., MG (Ret.) (2008). Notes from Lecture at Fort Campbell, Kentucky 11 March 2008. rdshadley@comcast.net.

Sherover, C. (Ed.). (1974). *The development of the democratic idea*. New York: Mentor Books.

Skinner, Quentin (1990) Thomas Hobbes on the proper significance of liberty: The Prothero Lecture. *Transactions of the Royal Historical Society*, Fifth Series. Vol.40, pp. 121-151.

Stinson, J. and Johnson, T. (1975). The Path-Goal Theory of Leadership: A partial test and suggested refinement. *The Academy of Management Journal*, Vol. 18, No. 2 (Jun., 1975), pp. 242-252.

Stogdill, R. (1981). *Stogdill's handbook of leadership*. (10th ed.) New York: The Free Press.

Stogdill, Ralph (1974). *Handbook of leadership*, Free Press, New York, New York. Retrieved 27 January 2007 from "The Leadership Box", by David Boje, revised 2003, http://cbae.nmsu.edu/~dboje/teaching/338/traits.htm)

Stokesbury, J. (1980). *A short history of World War II*. New York, William Morrow Co.

Stouffer, S. Et al. (1949) *Studies in Social Psychology in World War II : The American soldier: Adjustment during Army life, Volume I*. Princeton, New Jersey: Princeton University Press.

Stouffer, S. Et al. (1949) *Studies in Social Psychology in World War II : The American soldier: Combat and its aftermath, Volume II*. Princeton, New Jersey: Princeton University Press.

Themes, P. (1996). *Teaching leadership: Essays in theory and practice*. New York: Peter Lang Publishing, Inc.

Tienda, M. (2002) Demography and the social contract. *Demography*. VOL 39, Number 4, November 2002, pp. 587-616.

The Statistics Home Page. Retrieved 25 January 2007 from http://www.statsoft.com /textbook/stathome.html

U.S. Army (1990). FM 22-100 Military Leadership. United States Army. DOD Publications.

Weber, R. (1990). *Basic content analysis*. Sage Publications, London.

Wessely, S. (2006). Twentieth-century theories on combat motivation and breakdown. *Journal of Contemporary History*, 41(2), pp. 269-286.

White, B. (2007). *The nature of leadership: reptiles, mammals, and the challenge of becoming a great leader*. New York: AMACOM Books.

Yukl, G. (2006). *Leadership in organizations* (6th Edition). Upper Saddle River, NJ: Prentice Hall.

Yung, Christopher D. (2006). *Gators of Neptune.* Annapolis, MD: Naval Institute Press.

Zabecki, D. (Ed.) (1999) *World War II in Europe: An encyclopaedia.* New York: Garland Publishing.

Zabecki, D. (2005). Notes from unpublished interview on World War I study.

Zabecki, D. (2009). Notes from unpublished interview on World War II study.

Zaccaro, S. (2007). Trait—based perspectives of leadership. *American Psychologist Jan 2007, Vol. 62 Issue 1*, 6-16.

APPENDIX A

INTERVIEW MATERIAL

From the World War II 60 Executive Committee interviews conducted 4 June 2004 in Normandy, France.

Crispin, Frederick, Army Air Corps Navigator, 2nd Lieutenant
Interview conducted in France on 4 June 2004. Interview transcribed by Lisa A. Zafirov, April 2006, proofed by LTC Al Koenig, HQ First US Army, Ft. Gillem, Georgia

Williamson, Francis, Staff Sergeant, 82nd Airborne Division
Interview conducted in France by Sergeant Sepko on 4 June 2004. Interview transcribed by Lisa A. Zafirov, May 2006, proofread by LTC Alan R. Koenig, HQ First US Army, Ft. Gillem, Georgia

From an interview conducted in Elsenz, Germany of World War II Veterans by Michael D. Pierce.

Luchner, Max, Carpenter
Interview conducted 22 August 2007, Elsenz, Baden-Wuerttemberg, Germany.

Additional Source Consultants

Koenig, Alan, LTC (Ret.) PhD, Professor of Military History, University of Nebraska

-Omaha. World War II 60 Executive Committee, Historical Record Liaison.

Rush, Robert H., PhD, 31 August 2007, Assistant Director, Center for Military History, notes from email discussion on military leadership.

Zabecki, David T., MG, PhD, Executive Director World War II 60 Executive Committee, Europe, United States Army Europe, Heidelberg, Germany.

APPENDIX B

SOURCE MATERIAL INDEX

WORLD WAR II 60TH ANNIVERSARY OF D-DAY: AN ORAL HISTORY BY THOSE WHO WERE THERE

TABLE OF CONTENTS

PART I. ORAL HISTORIES FROM THE D-DAY INVASION
—Index of histories

A. Interviews

Balkom, Detachment Commander/Flight Control Officer, 66th Fighter Group, 9th Air Force, USAAF. Transcribed by LTC Alan R. Koenig, FA, USAR. {3881}

Brown, Harry, Corporal serving in World War II. Interviewed by Major Douglas Hendy. {6668}

Caliguerre, Frank, of Cleveland, Ohio. He was a crewman on USAAF cargo planes in the ETO. Transcribed by LTC Alan R. Koenig. {2167}

Collard, Pierre, a French soldier fighting in the Resistance LTC Millett translated from the French language, and LTC Alan R. Koenig. {1125}

Cook, Eugene jumped into Normandy with the 101st Airborne and later fought in Holland and in the Battle of the Bulge. Transcribed by LTC Alan R. Koenig. {1522}

Eudy, James R., 264th anti-tank company of the 66th Infantry Division (Black Panther). Transcribed by LTC Alan R. Koenig, FA, USAR. {824}

Franco, Arnold C., 9th Air Force, 3rd Radio Squadron, Mobile (G). Interview conducted by Major Douglas Hendy and transcribed by John T. Moore, Jr. {4763}

Goodall, Clifford Signalman, 2nd Class, US Navy, 7th Naval Beach Battalion, attached to the 6th Engineer Special Brigade for D-Day Invasion. Interview conducted by Major Douglas Hendy and transcribed by John T. Moore, Jr. {1709}

LaMoureux, Francis, served with the 508th parachute infantry regiment. Interviewed by Major Douglas Hendy. {8792}

Liberto, Joseph. Former infantryman turned graves registration specialist by the time of OPERATION OVERLORD. Transcribed by LTC Alan R. Koenig. {489}

Merriman, Paul. Staff Sergeant, 736th Field Artillery Battalion. <u>Note:</u> SGT Merriman provided extremely detailed information about duty in an artillery battalion in the ETO. He related that he had extensive documentation of his wartime experiences back in the United States. A copy of this documentation would be nice to have on file at the Military History Institute. Transcribed by LTC Alan R. Koenig. {5503}

Raymond, Walter T., CPL, assigned as an infantry squad leader with K Company, 315 Infantry Regiment, 79th Infantry Division during the Normandy Invasion. Interview conducted at the USO in Paris, France by Major Doug Hendy. {4676}

Roberts, Major General (retired) James M., aide to V Corps Commander Lieutenant General Walter Gerow. Interview conducted by Major James Hendy, 44th Military History Detachment, at Normandy in June 2004, and transcribed by LTC Alan R. Koenig. {2217}

Schein, Norman, Sergeant T4, 248th Engineer Battalion. Interviewer was Major Doug Hendy, USA. {2004}

Skorupa, Albert, First Engineers Special Brigade, Company C, 531st ESR Interview conducted at the USO in Paris, France, June 1, 2004 by Sergeant 1st Class, Sergeant Jason Lefavre 44th Military History Detachment. {737}

Smith, Everett W. a US Navy crewman, interviewed by LTC Alan R. Koenig (August 2004). *{310}*

Joseph Buckner Sullivan 50ᵗʰ General Hospital. Transcribed by Alan R. Koenig, LTC, FA, USAR. *{1264}*

Warfield, Joseph W. Half-track operator: 443rd Coast Artillery Battalion, 3rd Division. Interview conducted at the USO in Paris, France, June 2, 2004 by Staff Sergeant 1st Class, Sergeant Jason Lefavre 44th Military History Detachment. *{1799}*

Ziemer, Richard, Tech Sergeant. 94ᵗʰ Squadron (USAAF, presumably). He rode in C-47s that dropped paratroops into Normandy and then continued to fight thru France for eleven months. Transcribed by LTC Alan R. Koenig. *{345}*

Zwick, Harold, 203ʳᵈ Combat Engineers (demolitions/mine clearing), at Normandy Beachhead. Transcribed by LTC Alan R. Koenig. {720}

B. Transcribed Interviews (Near Finished Product)
Interviews transcribed by SGT Kenneth D. Hall

Abernathy, Milton, On a Clear Day You Can See Forever . . . *303ʳᵈ's Milton Abernathy's New Year's Eve Party at 16,000 Feet {287}*

Alley, Thomas, Two Years in the Making . . . *101ˢᵗ Airborne's Thomas Alley Got The Jump On Things {814}*

Ahumada, Albert J., MISSION: Capture Enemy Soldier Behind Lines . . . *V Corps' Albert J. Ahumada Floats in for Abduction {378}*

Anonymous . . . Landing with the 4ᵗʰ on the 6ᵗʰ to Join the 9ᵗʰ . . . *and the long way around to getting married {452}*

McCauley, Harold, Slaughter at Slapton Sands . . . 4th *ID's Harold McCauley's Voyage of Recovery {2486}*

McNamara, William G., And the World Watched the War . . . *Through the Eyes of William G. McNamara: War Correspondent {693}*

Miljeciv, Alexander G., Combat Arms Disadvantage . . . 4th *ID's Alexander G. Miljevic Faces Superior Firepower {438}*

Molinari, Peter, Waist Deep in War . . . 5th *ID's Peter Molinari Carried a Heavy Load* {989}

Murphy, Robert Martin, Distinguished Service at the La Fayette Bridge . . . *Robert Martin Murphy "Going First" with the 82*[nd] {701}

Peterson, Herschel, The Dawning Days of D-Day . . . 286th*'s Herschel Peterson Evades Wolfpack Action {816}*

Piper, Robert Martin, The Apple of the Enemy's Eye . . . 82nd *Airborne's Robert Martin Piper's Hornets Nest {345}*

Porcella, Thomas, Password: "Flash Thunder" . . . 82nd*'s Thomas Porcella's Flash with Death {643}*

Roderick, David, All American Kid . . . 4th *ID's David Roderick Goes to War at 16 {1000}*

Scanlon, Tom, Doctor Rebel with a Cause . . . 4th *ID Combat Medic Tom Scanlon, and the Many Trials and Trails Traveled {2341}*

Sellner, Cletus, "How are the Cincinnati *Cardinals* doing?" . . . 101st*'s Cletus Sellner Remembers the Enemy Imposters {1585}*

Scaglione, Philip, Swamp Rat to Maze Master . . . 29th *ID's Philip Scaglione Survives Snipers in the Trenches {424}*

Schlemmer, SGT Zane D., Denying Death and the Enemy Encompass . . . 82nd*'s SGT D. Zane Schlemmer and the Baptism of Fire {1023}*

Schreirer, Robert L., Ports of Call . . . *302nd's Robert L Schreirer Offloads the War Effort {702}*

Shearer, Charles, We Dropped in for a Drink . . . *439th TCG's Charles Shearer Gets Time to Know the Locals {441}*

Smolens, Irving, Operations Afoot . . . *4th ID's Irving Smolens Survives Slapton Sands {1664}*

Sellner, Cletus, "How are the Cincinnati *Cardinals* doing?" . . . *101st's Cletus Sellner Remembers the Enemy Imposters* {1585}

Sponheimer, Albert, Medic on the Move . . . *197th's Albert Sponheimer: Lifeguard Duty on Omaha Beach {912}*

Stadler, Jesse, From The Fith of Clyde to Bad Tolz and Back . . . *4th ID's Jesse Stadler Runs the War Gauntlet {847}*

Staruk, Walter, From Border to Border . . . *90th ID's Walter Staruk Communicated Across Europe {491}*

Stritto, Joe, Flight of the Damned . . . *Pilot Joe Stritto Glides into a Killing Field {471}*

Tate, Robert, Nowhere to Hide . . . *9th ID's Robert Tate and the Rommel Rematches {802}*

Thompson, Farrell, Going on the Air in Style . . . *U.S. Navy's Farrell Thompson Hits a German Mess Hall {323}*

Toniguzzo, Dante, The Modest Warrior . . . *82nd's Dante Toniguzzo Walked the Path of Greatness {460}*

Torre, Armand, The Old Warriors . . . *4th ID's Armand Torre Defies Death for Duty {793}*

Tucker, Will and Frank Bilich, Comrades in Arms . . . *82nd Airborne's Will Tucker and Frank Bilich Fight in Fellowship {1284}*

PART II. HISTORICAL ARTICLES FROM WWII 60 COMMITTEE

APPENDIX C

I. MAPS AND CHARTS

D-Day Map 1

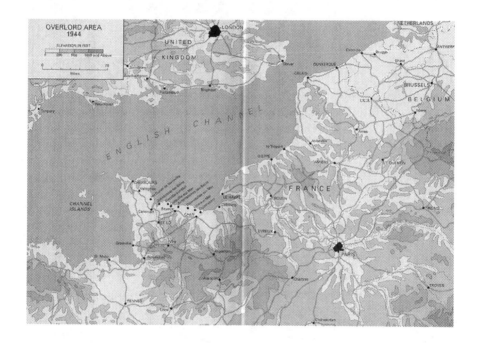

D-Day Map 2

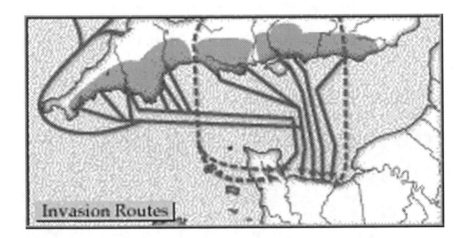

D-Day Map 3

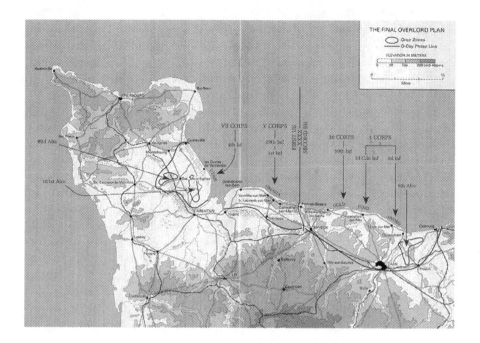

D-Day Map 4

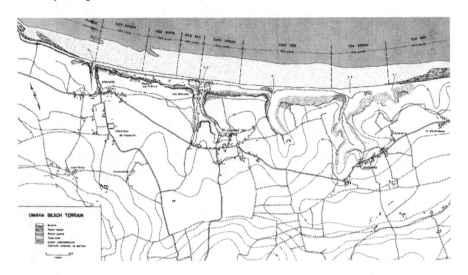

Map Source: http://www.internet-esq.com/ussaugusta/overlord/

APPENDIX C

II. PHOTOS

Photos of captured British Spitfires with German Markings

Reference: Private John Paulson's account of General Bradley being strafed at Omaha Beach in June 1944 (p. 186).

http://www.luftwaffe-experten.org/forums/index.php?showtopic=310